# THE HANDBOOK OF
# SAILING
# TECHNIQUES

GAIL BORDEN LIBRARY

# THE HANDBOOK OF
# SAILING
# TECHNIQUES

**TWAIN BRADEN**

**The Lyons Press**
**Guilford, CT 06437**
The Lyons Press is an imprint of The Globe Pequot Press

LAD 8/08
Use 5

First Lyons Press edition, 2003
Copyright © 2003 by Amber Books Ltd

ALL RIGHTS RESERVED. No part of this book may be reproduced or transmitted in any form by any means, electronic or mechanical, including photocopying and recording, or by any information storage and retrieval system, except as may be expressly permitted by the 1976 Copyright Act or in writing from the publisher. Requests for permission should be addressed to The Globe Pequot Press, P.O. Box 480, Guilford, CT 06437.

The Lyons Press is an imprint of The Globe Pequot Press.

Editorial and design by:
Amber Books Ltd
Bradley's Close
74–77 White Lion Street
London N1 9PF
www.amberbooks.co.uk

Project Editor: Michael Spilling
Design: Zoë Mellors
Illustrations: Tony Randell and Kevin Jones Associates

PICTURE CREDITS
Front cover: Popperfoto

Printed in Italy by Eurolitho S.p.A.

2   4   6   8   10   9   7   5   3   1

The Library of Congress Cataloging-in-Publication Data is available on file.

ISBN 1-58574-644-4

DISCLAIMER

Neither the author nor the publisher can accept any responsibility for any loss, injury, or damage caused as a result of the use of the survival techniques used in this book, nor for any prosecutions or proceedings brought or instituted against any person or body that may result from using the aforementioned survival techniques.

# Contents

# Introduction

**Standing at the tiller of a small sailboat – making way in a fresh breeze – is one of the most exhilarating pleasures available to us. Whether we are joined by good friends or solo, sailing is an aesthetic experience that we respond to on all levels.**

There's an air of freedom to sailing, a feeling of delight at the limitless possibilities that can be achieved by the simple adjustment of lines and a turn of the tiller. This book is intended to empower the novice sailor to seek out that joy, to be unintimidated by the fancy language or the awkward-looking equipment, and to explore the watery world.

There is no single book that can tell you all you need to know about handling a boat at sea. Practical experience in a variety of conditions will lead to good judgement, which is the most fundamental and useful tool available to any mariner, whether captain of an 230-m (800-ft) oil tanker or skipper of a 4-m (12-ft) sailing dinghy.

This book is intended to offer novice sailors about 90 per cent of the skills and knowledge needed to get started on managing their own boats, whether at sea or on a lake or other waterway. As for the other 10 per cent, common sense and experience will account for that.

*The Handbook of Sailing Techniques* offers a systematic breakdown of the skills needed for operating a sailboat. Throughout we have used as our model a 6-m (20-ft) daysailer with a sloop rig and inboard diesel engine, and a fibreglass hull with full keel, steered by a tiller. If this description does not fit your boat, no matter; this is the Everyman of sailboats, and you can adjust the information easily to fit your needs.

If you feel you are in danger of drowning in details, remember your ultimate goal: the feel of the tiller in your hand as the wind fills the sails and whisks you on your way.

# CHAPTER 1

# The ocean and harbour environment

**You do not need to be a meteorologist to understand how weather affects your boat. You should, however, make it a priority to be aware of your surroundings on a daily – and seasonal – basis.**

In this age of information, there is ample opportunity for gaining a clear picture of the day's weather - from the Internet, television, radio, and newspapers. But you should do more than look at a weather report on the morning of your sail: be aware of the weather - and prevailing conditions - for the week before you sail to put this day's forecast in context. Also, speak with other, more experienced mariners in your area. Find out how the tides work, where in relation to points of land the currents exist, where the prevailing winds are known to blow from, where the swells are large.

However, none of this information will help you unless you make an effort to

## Weather patterns

Being aware of daily and seasonal weather patterns will lead to greater understanding – and peace of mind for enjoying a day's sail.

Make sure that you always obtain the day's forecast before heading out.

determine the conditions on a regular basis. Weather is both global and local in scale. Understanding how global weather works is a start; add to that a knowledge of the rhythms of your particular region. As Alan Watts, a British forecaster and author of numerous books, wrote in *The Weather Handbook*:'Listen to the forecasts, note what they say and then use your own knowledge to refine the details for your own area.' In other words, if you hear on the radio that it's raining outside, don't always take their word for it. Go outside and look at the sky!

This chapter is not a definitive guide to the science of weather. It is a starting point only, intended to provide the novice sailor with enough knowledge to begin sailing as soon as possible. Where this falls short of providing a full description of weather phenomena, the reader is directed to other sources for further information. The chapter provides information on weather at sea – including information on tides and tidal currents – but is applicable to freshwater sailing as well.

## THE LOGBOOK

Weather is fickle, changeable, and three-dimensional. But it can be observed and certain patterns then discerned, and these can be of use to the mariner. The single most important tool for the mariner is the logbook. Understanding weather requires observation, but observation is somewhat limited in value without a written record. Take the time to record the weather – every day and sometimes several times a day – and you will build up a store of observations and their context. With such knowledge comes the ability to make decisions.

Record the forecast. If the weather radio is calling for southwest winds from 10–15 knots, write this down. Note when the tide will be high and low, and whether there are any local anomalies such as thunderstorms or squalls expected. Once you have recorded this, you now have a frame of reference for the day's weather.

Look at the sky. Write down what you see by using a cloud identifier or simply by describing the physical nature of the clouds. Note the degree of cloud cover. Is the sky completely covered by clouds, or just partially?

Note the direction of the wind. Stand over your compass, feeling the wind on your face, and determine where it's coming from. Look down at the compass. You should already be aware of the weather's prevailing conditions. How does the day's weather compare to the

## Your logbook

Log the weather forecast in your boat log. During the day, record the actual weather conditions you experience, including cloud cover and wind direction and velocity.

## Watching the weather

Storms and squalls can develop quickly. By monitoring weather forecasts, you will be aware of the the conditions that can lead to dangerous weather activity.

prevailing conditions? If prevailing summer winds are from the south, what does it mean if you observe the wind to be blowing from the east? (This is not a trick question – it might mean that a change is in the air, bringing moisture or foul weather.) Many boats are equipped with a wind-angle indicator (windvane) and anemometer at the top of the mast. A glance at the dial in the cockpit will give you this information, too. Write it down.

Note the sea state. Are there swells from an offshore storm? What about whitecaps? If your cove or anchorage is sheltered and not indicative of where you will be sailing for the day, it may be prudent to gain a clear picture of open-water conditions. This can be viewed firsthand by observing the water from a headland or beach, or by checking the Internet. Many weather sites offer real-time weather conditions, including wave height, that are recorded by large weather buoys anchored offshore. The buoys transmit information – often on an hourly basis.

Like every tool aboard a boat, a logbook is useful only if it used and understood. Simply buying a logbook and entering your boat's name on the inside cover, then slipping it onto your bookshelf will not provide you with the knowledge you need. An added benefit to a well-kept log is that it provides a written record of your adventures. One of the great pleasures of the sailing life is recounting these tales from the security of an armchair on a cold winter's night.

## THE SUN AND THE WIND

Weather begins with the sun. Its warmth is responsible for creating convection currents on the earth's surface, forcing air masses to circulate around the atmosphere. The mixing of these masses in local areas – along with global effects of warm air churning from the equator and cold air tumbling down from the poles – generates a side effect called wind.

Wind, which can blow from any direction of the compass, blows across the top of the water and creates waves through friction. If a wind blows from one direction for great periods of time across water that is uninterrupted by land masses, then very large waves, called swells, form. The linear distance that wind blows across the water's surface is called 'fetch' – picture the trade winds blowing across the tropical regions of the world, blowing steadily for months on end from a single direction. As swells are formed over long periods, over thousands of miles of fetch, they can often oppose waves that are formed by more local effects. Seas in these conditions are described as 'confused'.

Understanding the relationship between the wind and waves is important to the sailor for several reasons. Sailing in confused seas

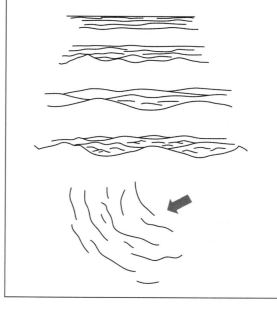

### Reading the waves

Look closely at the surface of the water. When the wind blows, you can actually see its effect on the waves. Little wavelets are formed on the leading edge of wind gust.

# Cloud recognition: some types

**Cirrus**

**Altostratus**

**Cirrostratus**

**Nimbostratus**

**Cirrocumulus**

**Cumulus**

**Altocumulus**

**Cumulonimbus**

# Know your clouds

Knowing the Latin names of the clouds is far less important than the act of observing the clouds and their physical properties. Clouds are indicators of certain weather conditions, however. Knowing the difference between the weather conditions that exist when cirrus clouds are present and those that exist in the vicinity of cumulonimbus will come with practice. Recognizing the various shapes of clouds and their habits will be another tool in your knowledge of maintaining a boat.

## 1. Cirrus

Cirrus clouds, and all their different forms, are the highest clouds. These are the wispy clouds that are often transparent; the sun can sometimes be seen right through them, shining through the haze. Cirrus clouds are actually tiny ice crystals, which can move swiftly through the upper atmosphere.

## 2. Cirrostratus

If cirrus clouds are light and wispy, then cirrostratus clouds are wispy and layered, lying across large portions of the sky in thin blankets – 'stratus' means layer. The sun may still be visible thorough this layer, often shining through the haze or accompanied by a halo. This layer of clouds is an indicator of an approaching storm.

## 3. Cirrocumulus

Cirrocumulus clouds are high and wispy, but they appear more often in clumps than cirrostratus. Change is in the air, either indicating a system that has just gone by or one that is approaching.

## 4. Altocumulus

Altocumulus clouds appear as heavier, lower clouds than altostratus. Altocumulus can produce 'mackerel sky', a layer of well-defined cirrocumulus clouds, appearing as a long, scalelike pattern that can portend lousy weather, especially if accompanied by winds from the northeast to southeast quadrant (or the opposite quadrant in the Southern Hemisphere).

## 5. Altostratus

Altostratus clouds are a low, dense layer that will bring rain if they continue to thicken.

## 6. Nimbostratus

Nimbostratus clouds are the dense, mid-level clouds that are responsible for dumping heavy, prolonged bouts of rain in both winter and summer. They are solid layers of cloud, dense with moisture.

## 7. Cumulus

Cumulus clouds are dense, puffy and well defined. These are the summer-day clouds that you observe moving slowly across the sky while lying on your back in a field of grass or on the deck of a sun-drenched sailboat. The clouds are textured, dark on the bottom, and with shadowy clumps visible along the sides. They indicate fair weather in a stable air mass.

## 8. Cumulonimbus

Cumulonimbus clouds are the dense, stacked clouds associated with thunderstorms or unstable air masses. A mariner who sees these thunderheads on the horizon should watch the clouds for ominous developments. When associated with a large anvil head and dark swathes of cloud in layers along the bottom, they are a good indicator of an approaching thunderstorm. Watch for shifting winds as these cells advance across the water. Such wind and rain squalls can often be seen well in advance. Consider shortening or dousing sail, or even heading for a secure anchorage.

## Beaufort scale

Force 1    Force 2    Force 3    Force 4    Force 5

### Force 1
Light air. The wind is blowing at 1–3 knots, causing ripples on the surface of the water.

### Force 2
Light breeze. The wind is blowing at 4–6 knots, enough to produce small wavelets, the crests of which do not break.

### Force 3
Gentle breeze. The wind is at 7–10 knots, creating large wavelets, the crests of which are beginning to break. A few whitecaps may be visible, but these do not dominate the sea surface.

### Force 4
Moderate breeze. The wind blows at 11–16 knots. Small waves begin to form, and these are 0.6–1.2m (2–4ft) in height. There are now numerous whitecaps.

### Force 5
Fresh breeze. The wind is now blowing at 17–21 knots, forming waves that are 1.2–2.1m (4–7ft). There are numerous whitecaps, some of which are sending spray into the air.

can be uncomfortable and dangerous, as the boat and crew cannot develop a rhythm. Also, it is important to realize that strong winds, which are associated with local weather effects such as squalls, may not be accompanied by large waves because the weather cell may blow through quickly, meaning there is not enough time to build large waves. A wind that blows over a land mass – an offshore wind – will not create large waves close to shore, no matter how long it blows, as the fetch is short. And yet, further offshore, this same wind might generate larger waves.

An example of this effect is pronounced on many tropical islands of the Caribbean and Pacific, which have 'windward' and 'leeward' sides. The windward sides are continually battered by large swells, and any harbours on this side will have entrances that are treacherous for small boats; the leeward sides are more sheltered, offering gentler entrances and quiet anchorages. The city of San Juan on Puerto Rico, which is on the east side of the island, and the town of Havana on the north side of Cuba are constantly slammed by large ocean waves that are the result of trade winds blowing across a long fetch. Both of their harbours are open to the sea, which means that swells pile up at the mouth, making the entrance a difficult approach for all vessels.

## THUNDERSTORMS
Thunderstorms, which can be either the result of isolated storm cells or the harbinger of a large frontal system, can be fierce and

## Beaufort scale (continued)

Force 6     Force 7     Force 8     Force 9     Force 10

### Force 6

Strong breeze. The wind blows at 22–27 knots, creating whitecaps everywhere.

### Force 7

Near gale. The wind blows at 28–33 knots. Seas are from 2.4–3.6m (8–12ft) in height. Foam begins to blow in the air. Whitecaps are being blown apart by the wind, forming long, white streaks on the sea's surface.

### Force 8

Gale. Wind speeds are 34–40 knots. Seas can build to 4.2–6m (14–20ft) in height. The surface of the water is streaked with foam.

### Force 9

Strong gale. Wind speeds are 41–47 knots, forming high waves more than 6m (20ft) in height. Spray begins to limit visibility, especially for small boats.

### Force 10

Storm. The wind is blowing at 48–55 knots, building seas to 6–8.2m (20–27ft). The crests of the waves overhang. The sea surface is coloured almost uniformly white with spray and foam. Visibility is significantly reduced.

### Force 11

Violent storm. Winds blow at 56–63 knots. Waves are 9.1–15m (30–50ft). Spray and foam fill the air.

### Force 12

Hurricane – Category 1. Wind speeds are 64–71 knots. The air is filled with driving spray; the sea surface is white. Visibility is near zero.

explosive, packing gusty winds and dropping torrential rains.

But the conditions that make for the possibility of thunderstorms are well understood. The mariner need not live in fear of a thunderstorm leaping out of the skies at any moment, although it is easy to be surprised by a thunderstorm if you are not paying attention to the weather. Thunderstorms can often be seen well in advance. Sheets of rain – appearing as veils of grey that stretch from the sea surface to the base of the cloud layer – can often be seen from many miles away. The winds associated with such storm cells can also be seen, advancing across the water in the direction the storm is moving, often blowing spray and streaking the water's surface.

## BEAUFORT SCALE

The Beaufort Scale, named after the British naval officer Sir Francis Beaufort (1774-1857), who developed the system, is a handy gauge to determine the velocity of the wind by studying the surface of the water. It is measured on a scale from 0 (flat calm) to Force 12 (hurricane). While somewhat dated, the Beaufort Scale can be used as a quick check on the weather as the sailor studies the water's surface. It may make sense to use Beaufort measurements in the logbook.

The Beaufort Scale uses specific language to describe the wind speed and its effect on the sea's surface:

- 'Wavelets' are precursors to actual 'waves'.
- A 'breeze' is a technical term, describing a wind that, depending on how it is defined, might be blowing anywhere between 4 and 27 knots.
- The descriptions of wave height pertain to situations where the wind is blowing continuously with unlimited fetch. In the open ocean, a 20-knot breeze might build waves that are as high as 2m (7ft). The same 20-knot breeze blowing across a small lake or harbour might produce only a few whitecaps, as there is not enough fetch to build the waves over a long period.

## LIGHTNING

Lightning is a danger to anyone who spends time in the out-of-doors. While lightning strikes on sailboats are relatively rare, they do occur, often with tragic results. It is prudent to equip the top of your mast with a lightning rod, which is 'grounded' to the water by a wire running down a shroud or stay. However, there is no foolproof method for avoiding lightning altogether, and you should seek shelter – in other words, anchorage – immediately if lightning is observed. If caught out in a lightning storm, crew members should avoid being close to metal objects, particularly shrouds and stays. Remember, too, that electronic equipment – GPS, radar, and sailing instruments – can be destroyed by electric storms; disconnect this equipment if a severe storm is approaching.

The proximity of an electrical storm can be estimated by counting the number of

## Reading your barometer

A barometer is an excellent tool for weather observation. You need to consult it regularly, every hour, for it to be useful. You need to know the change in barometric pressure, not just the pressure itself.

seconds between a lightning flash and the sound of its thunder. Divide the number of seconds by five to derive the distance, in statute miles, of the storm. A thunderclap that sounds 20 seconds after the lightning is observed is four statute miles away from your location. This method can become confused as the storm approaches, however, as it may be difficult to determine which thunderclap goes with which lightning flash.

If the conditions for thunderstorms – warmth and humidity – are prevalent, listen to the weather forecasts with increased vigilance. Forecasters will describe the presence and severity of storms with regularity.

## BAROMETER

A barometer measures atmospheric pressure at any given time of day. Like most tools that observe the weather, the barometer is of limited value without context. You need to know what the barometer has been doing in previous hours, sometimes for as many as 12–24 hours, to understand the significance of its reading. Some barometers record the readings over time, allowing the user to see a printed record of the pressure over several hours and even several days.

If the pressure stays fairly steady for several hours on end, the weather will be markedly different than if you observe the barometer to be falling, say, one millibar every hour over the course of six hours. In general, when using a barometer, it is important to know that rapid change in barometric pressure is a harbinger of powerful weather systems at work: severe storms or fronts are in the vicinity. Note, too, that the closer the pressure gradients are on a weather map, the stronger the wind is going to blow.

This does not mean that the barometer needs to be plummeting for the winds to be blowing hard. If the barometer is steady and the winds are still howling, this probably means that the low pressure system causing the winds is stationary.

The barometer user should also be aware of 'diurnal change', a daily flux in pressure that can be more than one millibar in a six-hour period.

Most weather maps and reports report barometric pressure in millibars, making a barometer that measures in 'inches of mercury' less useful than one with a millibar gauge. (One millibar is equal to .03 inches of mercury; one inch equals 33.86 millibars. The standard atmospheric pressure of 1013.2 millibars is equal to 29.92 inches.)

Any boat that sails offshore, which means overnight passagemaking, should be equipped with a barometer. Just because you are not an offshore sailor does not mean that a barometer is not useful. It just might make more sense to mount it on your kitchen wall as opposed to your boat if you sail a 60-m (20-ft) daysailer.

## FOG

The bane of every navigator's existence, fog is common in most temperate coastal waters when cold water intermingles with warm air. Navigating in fog tries the patience of even the most experienced sailor for the simple reason that it is a bit like sailing blindfolded. You cannot see a thing, yet all the rules of safe watchkeeping still apply – you must keep track of your position, watch out for other boats, and avoid running aground. Peering through the fog is always exhausting, and this fatigue will not help.

But just because you cannot see more than a few feet beyond the bow of your boat does not mean you have to hide under the covers. You can still see your sails; you can still see within a small distance in all directions. And you can still hear and smell – senses that are not to be underestimated on a boat. Heading out for a day's sail in congested shipping lanes or a busy harbour in heavy fog may not be advisable, but if fog rolls in while you're under way, there's no need to panic.

So, what causes fog? Fog forms when two air masses of different temperatures come into contact. Fog forms because an air mass has become cooled below its dew point. An air mass' dew point is the point – the temperature – at which the air is saturated with water. When this occurs by rapid cooling, the air mass contains fog. Picture mountain valleys in the early morning, the hollows clutching the warm, moist air from the previous the day, while the chill of the night sits atop, forming fog. Picture, too, the cold, northern waters lapping at the shores of Maine or Scotland in early summer, when the cold water chills the air immediately above.

There are many different types of fog – advection fog, radiation fog, and sea smoke – but they are all formed by the same basic function: the interaction between air masses of different temperature and humidity.

### Navigating in fog

Navigating through fog is not impossible; it simply requires heightened awareness of your surroundings and your situation. An old joke in Maine, where foggy summers are notorious among boaters, describes 'potato navigation'. The navigator guiding her vessel through fog continuously lobs potatoes off the bow, straight ahead of the vessel: when the potato makes a splash, keep sailing; when the potato is heard thumping against something hard, it is time to tack. However, there are tools other than a bushel of potatoes and a good throwing arm, and these are useful to the fogbound navigator. The first is the sounding lead. Checking the depth of the water can help to locate your position; compare your soundings against your charts.

Proceed slowly. Motor-driven vessels can simply reduce speed by throttling back, but sailboats need to be more creative. Sailing with a reef in the mainsail, or striking one of the sails altogether, will slow your headway. You don't want to proceed so slowly that you lose steerage, but nor do you want to proceed through thick fog at a boat's full speed.

Keep a careful lookout. If you are accustomed to having the helmsman as the only lookout, consider posting a dedicated crew member to the role of lookout in foggy conditions. Have the person either sitting or standing on the foredeck, or, if this is impractical, at least oriented in such a position as to be the first person to see other vessel or hazards. Remember that the traffic rules suggest that we avoid – if at all possible – an *in extremis* turn to port. In other words, if you see a vessel loom suddenly out of the fog, your first instinct should be to effect an immediate turn to starboard. (This rule is compatible with the general traffic rule of passing other vessels port-to-port.) However, if a turn to starboard will only make matters worse, by no means should you turn to starboard. Only you can make the call during the actual moment of manoeuvring, but do remember the general guidance.

Use sound signals. According to the International Rules of the Road, a sailboat proceeding in restricted visibility – either fog or heavy rain – should sound one prolonged blast on its horn followed by two short blasts every two minutes. A sailboat has an edge over power-driven vessels in fog: if you do not have an engine running and you are positioned outside on deck, as opposed to within an enclosed wheelhouse, you can hear a whole lot better than the crew of a powerboat. Use this to your advantage by paying close attention to sound signals, especially those that seem to be coming from forward of your beam, as these are the objects (lighthouses, whistle buoys, or other vessels) that you are likely to encounter as you continue on your course.

If you are under way when fog rolls in and envelops your boat, you will probably see it coming. In anticipation of fog, be sure to grab a last-minute visual fix, taking magnetic bearings off several objects and transferring the information to a chart. From this position, keep a careful dead reckoning as you proceed through the fog to your destination.

Sailboats do not have right of way over other vessels in fog. A sailboat proceeding in fog should not barrel along on its merry course assuming that other vessels will give way.

In short, listen carefully for sound signals at all times. Proceed slowly. Avoid turning to port to prevent collision with another vessel.

## TIDES

The effects of the rise and fall of the tides are apparent in all parts of the world's oceans, although sometimes in drastically different amounts. In general, there is greater tidal range (the difference in height between high and low tide) in higher latitudes. In the tropics, for example, there can be as little as 30cm (12in) or less of tidal height, whereas in many parts of the United States, Canada, and Northern Europe, there can be tidal heights in excess of 3m (10ft). Thankfully, extreme tides, such as those found in the Bay of Fundy in Canada, where they can be as high as 12m (40ft), are extremely rare.

The force of the tide is generated by the gravitational pull of the moon and the sun as earth moves through its orbit and spins on its axis. While there are average tidal heights, each high and low tide is slightly different in height than the one before and the one following. This is because the sun and moon and earth position themselves in such a way as to apply greater pulling force at a given time and less force at others.

Spring tides – which have nothing to do with spring, the season – are caused when the moon and sun align around the earth, combining their forces to create more extreme tides: higher high tides and lower low tides. There are two positions that the sun and moon can take to create spring tides: the first, when the sun and moon are aligned on the same side as the earth, pulling together; and the second, when they are on opposite sides, with the earth in between. In both instances, the pulling power of these heavenly bodies combines to make stronger tides. Spring tides occur twice per month – during the full moon and new moon.

Neap tides are a period of less extreme tidal range. They occur during periods when the sun and moon are pulling in perpendicular directions, each reducing the effects of the other one on the earth's tides. During neap tides, there are lower high tides and higher low tides. Neap tides occur twice a month, during the first and third quarter of the moon's phase.

Tide is also affected by geography. Local conditions, such as broad bays with narrow entrances or large shallow areas, can play with the effects of the tide, making more or less extreme tidal change. The best way to understand these effects in your area is to speak directly with other sailors and read the local guides.

## Tides and charts

Soundings on charts – in other words, the printed depths – typically indicate the depth of the water at what is called 'mean lower low water'. This confused expression is nothing more than the surveyor's attempt to make it less likely for the navigator to run aground. 'Mean lower low water' refers to the mean of the lowest tides. In other words, surveyors took their soundings at low water, then used the lowest ones to derive a mean number. Generally, therefore, when you sail over shallow water at low tide, the depth of the water will still be somewhat deeper than

## Determining the forecast

Most developed countries offer nonstop weather forecasts over dedicated VHF channels. The exact channel will vary with local areas.

the number indicated on your chart – unless, of course, you sail over the shallows at a period of extreme spring tide. It is possible to find less water than what is printed on the chart, but this is statistically improbable.

This is not to say, however, that you should assume that surveyors have left you a small margin for error and that you can therefore cut corners while navigating. Always plan to leave plenty of water below your keel. Even if your boat draws only 1m (3ft) and the charted depth shows 1.2m (4ft), you might be sailing across this area at low tide when a swell is running. A 60-cm (2-ft) swell, for example, would drop your boat like a melon onto the bottom as your boat dropped into the trough of the wave.

Bridge clearances are also given on charts and publications for times of mean high water – for the same reason. The clearance given will very probably be the least amount of clearance between the surface of the water and the underside of the bridge (at the highest point). Again, take no chances. Be sure to have a careful measurement of your mast's height, and read your chart carefully. Take extra caution not to confuse vertical clearance with horizontal clearance – these figures are printed side by side.

## Tide terminology

When the tide is coming in, this is called the flood; when the tide is outgoing, it is known as the ebb.

The movement of water in a horizontal direction as a result of the tide is called tidal current. Tidal current can be associated with either an ebb or flood tide cycle, and it is therefore referred to as being an ebb or flood current.

Diurnal tides are when there is only one high tide and one low tide in a 24-hour

## High tide

When you tie up to a seawall at high tide, you will want to be sure that the lines that you use have enough slack so that they will not become too taut as the tide falls. Never leave a boat unattended if you are unsure of the tidal range where you are moored.

# Low tide

If your vessel cannot be safely grounded out, you will want to be sure not to leave your boat in such an area. (Your chart gives depth of low water.) If your vessel can safely be grounded, you should know the nature of the bottom before letting your vessel ground.

period. Semi-diurnal tides are when an area experiences two high tides and two low tides in a 24-hour period.

Mixed tides are found in several parts of the world, including on the West Coast of the United States. High tides alternate between being higher and lower with a low tide in between. This is actually not as confusing as it may sound. The high and low tide cycle is roughly the same as in places of semi-diurnal tidal areas, except that with mixed tides the height of the tides varies more from one high and low to the next.

Slack tide is the period at high and low tide when the current is neither ebbing nor flooding. It is still, or slack. This period is typically about 15 minutes in duration.

Note that a tidal wave has nothing to do with the tide. It is more accurately known as a 'tsunami' and is a massive wave or series of waves caused by tremors, volcanic eruption, or subsidence on the ocean floor.

## Waves and tides

Tidal current can have an extreme effect on wave height and shape. An ebb tidal current running against the direction of the wind will produce steep, choppy waves because the movement of the water is opposing the wind, creating more friction. This effect is also common at river bars, where swiftly flowing rivers meet the sea.

Extreme caution should be practised when navigating these areas, which can be plagued with steep, breaking waves with a short interval. Seaway with these conditions can be dangerous to the boat and uncomfortable to the crew. Waves can break on deck. Effects of seasickness will be more pronounced as the boat is tossed haphazardly in the waves.

## Crossing a bar

A river bar can produce large breaking waves at the entrance, a result of the flow of the river and the waves of the ocean coming together.

These can be exacerbated by a variety of factors, including wind strength and direction, stage of the tide, and geographical features.

## COMPUTERS AND THE WEATHER

Computers have revolutionized weather forecasting and weather information management. Computers can access the Internet and keep track of your position; they can perform all your navigational exercises, including set and drift equations, and even celestial navigation. Indeed, the amount of information available to the cautious mariner is staggering. Today, we can access a detailed surface analysis from a computer, gathering surface temperatures, wave heights, wind speeds, and visibility reports from automated buoys.

But, just like a barometer that is useless unless it is read on a regular basis, a computer is useful only if it is understood, used properly, and used with regularity.

Weather-related websites available for the mariner can be divided in two categories: those that provide free weather information, including forecasts, current conditions, and other real-time data; and those that charge for customized service. Private meteorologists who offer these services typically provide a detailed look at the weather for a particular offshore passage, offering a description of both the currents and 'weather window' to expect. Someone planning a trip from England to the Azores or New England to Bermuda, for example, might confer with a meteorologist to determine the best conditions for a departure. Weather forecasts are considered highly accurate within about 48 hours. For trips that will take longer, weather experts can supply routing information, explaining where low- and high-pressure systems are located, and even recommending routes for the boat to take. Contact with these shore-based services can be done via satellite, either by e-mail or voice communication. High-seas communication can also be performed via HAM or single-sideband radio.

Sites that offer general weather information for free can be just as useful, but require more initiative on the part of the user:

- The Royal Meteorological Society in the United Kingdom is a boon to the weather enthusiast or amateur sailor, providing links for forecasts, satellite and radar images, and detailed information on all weather-related activities. Find it at www.royal-met-soc.org.uk.
- In the United States, the National Atmospheric Administration (NOAA) provides satellite images of much of the world, radar images of select areas, tidal information, and detailed forecasts for many parts of the world. Coverage spans

the US coastline, including the Gulf of Mexico, the eastern half of the North Pacific Ocean, and the western half of the North Atlantic Ocean. Find it at www.noaa.gov. For the National Weather Service, go to www.weather.gov.

Many sites ask for a zip code or the nearest city to provide a detailed look at a specific geographical area. More specific coverage and weather interpretation can be derived through the Marine Prediction Center.

● Another handy site for weather-related information is the French weather service, Meteo France. Find it at www.meteo.fr.

## Power in your lap

**A laptop computer can be used at home and on a boat for weather forecasting, navigation, and myriad other boat-related tools.**

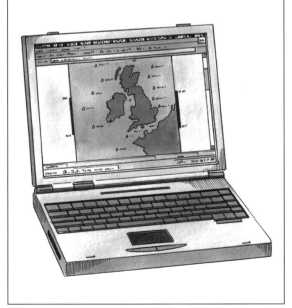

Many weather websites offer raw weather data, which is rife with arcane meteorological symbols. Much of this weather language can be learned with the assistance of a weather book and some common sense. There are also numerous software programs that are intended to interpret this information into a usable format, providing wind speeds, wave heights, and wind direction to the navigator.

Although most small-boat sailors prefer to keep their computers at home, you should not forget that computers can be used on board as well. Many software packages are available for a navigator who wants to interface sailing instruments into his laptop or combine weather information with navigational charts for voyage planning. Be sure to use a stable power source on a boat, as navigating by computer means being reliant on electrical power. If you do not have a sufficient power source available on the boat, ensure that your computer's batteries are fully charged before you sail. Paper charts should always be used as the primary source of information, however.

Many sailors nowadays choose to use handheld computers. Weather information and navigational software can be downloaded at home from the Internet, and the computer can then be taken aboard and referred to in the cockpit. Some of these computers can be fitted with an inbuilt GPS receiver, making real-time navigation exercises a cinch. You should consider protecting your investment with purpose-built waterproof bags.

The choice to be or not to be a wired sailor need not be an all-or-nothing decision. If you are a technophile, the weather and navigational software programs available today are straightforward and easy to use. And if you are the type of person who views computers as a menace, you should still bear in mind that there is plenty of easily derived weather information available online.

# CHAPTER 2

# Boat anatomy

**Knowing the parts of the boat, including common terms for various equipment and their uses, is an important first step in building a solid foundation of seamanship skills.**

True, sailing terms often sound quaint at first, but using the terminology knowledgeably often makes the difference between a safe boat and one that is chaotic and unpredictable. Take the time to learn the terms and use the language on your boat. In moments of high excitement – when a docking manoeuvre goes wrong or when it is time to reef the sails before a squall – you'll be glad your crew knows what to reach for, which lines to pull, and how to go about a given task with precision.

Whether you choose to sail a 2.5-m (8-ft) dinghy or a 15-m (50-ft) yacht, the principles are the same. Knowing which boat best fits your interest (and wallet) is the first step in entering the world of sailing; equal enjoyment can be had in all manner of sailing craft, large or small.

Throughout this book, we will assume, when discussing parts of a boat, an example of a modestly sized daysailer, some 6m (20ft)

in length; it has two sails, a mainsail and a jib (in other words, it's a sloop); and it has a large cockpit, is steered by a tiller, and has a fibreglass hull with a full keel. One final point: this boat is powered by a small, inboard diesel engine. For such a small boat, an inboard engine might be a rarity – a boat of this size might be fitted with an outboard or have no engine at all – but this will this example will be useful for discussion. Modifications on this design – different rigs, different hull design, alternative power choices such as an outboard motor or oars – will be possible without changing the basic idea of how to maintain and handle a small sailing vessel.

An important difference between large vessels and small ones is that everything happens more quickly on small craft: the smaller and lighter the boat is, the jerkier the motion will be. That is not necessarily a function of pure speed; many large boats are capable of breathtaking speeds. Again, what you choose to sail should be a function of the type of sailing you want. Pure speed or leisurely, aesthetic meandering? Something for a day's picnic on an island or a boat to live on?

## KEELS – FIXED OR DEPLOYABLE

The first distinction to understand about boats is the difference between those with a keel and those without. A sailboat must convert energy from the wind into forward motion, and, to do this, it must counteract the sideways force of the wind. (For a complete discussion of the mechanics of sailing, see Chapter 7.) A sailboat therefore needs to have a deep profile, called a keel, below the waterline. A keel fulfils several functions, preventing the boat from side-slipping (making leeway), and keeping it upright against the heeling force of the wind. Generally speaking, the deeper and heavier the keel, the stiffer a boat will be – that is, less prone to heeling over when the breeze becomes strong. Keels are often composite structures, built from fibreglass (or wood on a wooden boat; steel on a steel boat), then fitted with lead or iron at the bottom for ballast.

A fin keel is one that drops nearly straight down from the bottom of the boat. Fin keels can be fitted to both displacement and planing hulls. Other boats have long, full keels that run nearly the length of the hull. Directional stability – the ability of a given boat to maintain a steady course – is a function of the lateral area below the waterline. A boat with a narrow, fin keel might be a better performer in terms of speed and agility than a boat with a long, deep keel, but it will also be more skittish, prone to be knocked about by small waves.

Boats that lack a full, fixed keel use a centreboard or daggerboard to keep the boat from making too much leeway. A centre-board – also called a swing keel on larger boats – is stored within a 'trunk' and lowered

into the water by a pennant, a length of soft line or steel cable. Centreboards swing on a single axis and drop down, sometimes several feet deep, below the hull. Care should be taken to avoid grounding a boat with the centreboard in the lowered position because this can cause stress on the connection between the centreboard and the trunk. Centreboard boats make good daysailers for people who want to enjoy the thrill of a sail-boat without giving up the convenience of a vessel that can be easily trailered, hauled onto a beach, or nosed around in shallow water.

Daggerboards, like centreboards, are deployable keels; they do not swivel, however, but are dropped straight into the water through a vertical trunk.

Some small sailing vessels use 'leeboards' to counteract leeway; leeboards, one per side, are deployed alongside the vessel, usually swivelling on a bar that runs across the beam of the boat. (Leeboards were popular on traditional Dutch sailing barges and other specialized designs.)

## HULLS

To generalize, the hulls of sailboats can be divided into two categories: displacement and planing. Loosely put, planing hulls are meant to skip across the water's surface, whereas a displacement hull travels through the water, literally displacing water as it moves. As one would think, displacement vessels tend to be slower than their more skittish counterparts, but there are advantages to both designs.

Displacement vessels are the more traditional design, having a rounded, full shape below the waterline. Picture the Gloucester fishing schooners and the Bristol Channel pilot cutters of the nineteenth century: these were deep-draft, heavy boats, built for going to sea in the harshest of circumstances. Today, displacement vessels are the cruising vessels and the daysailers that can be used loaded with gear. Overall

# Parts of the boat

This sloop-rigged sailboat is the 'model boat' used for this book. It is some 6m (20ft) long and has a fibreglass hull, an inboard engine, and a sloop rig. This last means that it has two sails: a mainsail and a jib. It can be steered by either a tiller or a wheel.

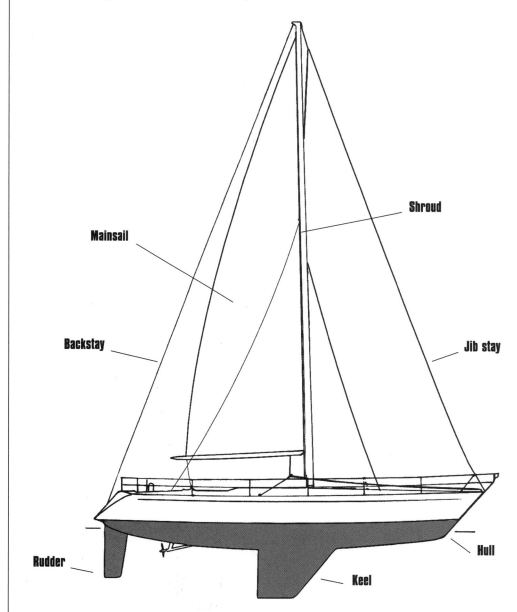

Shroud

Mainsail

Backstay

Jib stay

Rudder

Hull

Keel

speed performance is less of a concern for owners of displacement vessels, who opt instead for comfort and practicality. There are ways, of course, to make displacement vessels go fast, but their overall speed is restricted by the fact that they are forced to displace the water as they move ahead. Hence 'hull speed', the theoretical limit to how fast a displacement vessel can go and itself a function of the boat's waterline length. To determine a displacement boat's hull speed, first determine the square root of the length of the waterline and multiply this number by 1.34. A displacement boat with a 6-m (20-ft) waterline, for example, will have a theoretical hull speed of almost 6 knots.

Many of today's popular daysailers – Sunfish, Lasers, and 420s – have planing hulls. The vessels practically skip across the tops of the waves and are therefore not

## The gaff rig

Gaff-rigged vessels were common in the nineteenth century. Although more cumbersome to handle because of the large number of lines required to set, strike, and trim sails, they are enjoyable rigs because of their versatility.

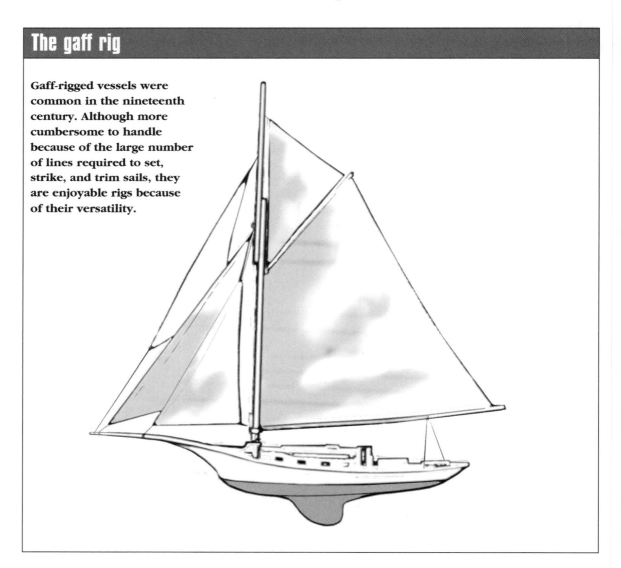

slaves to the laws of hull speed. Indeed, some designs can achieve speeds of more than 30 knots. As would be expected, these are the race boats that compete in events such as the Vendee Globe, Around Alone, and Volvo Ocean Race.

## Multihulls

Centuries ago, island colonists of the South Pacific discovered the advantages of using more than one hull to whisk them the vast distances between the islands. Separating a hull into two (or even three) parts brings two advantages: stability and speed.

When a monohull sailing vessel is heeled by the wind, it must be stabilized, both by the width of its hull and by the depth and weight of its keel. Inevitably – and no matter the design – there comes a point at which it becomes impractical to add more weight or more beam. Separating the hulls effectively doubles or triples the beam, which exponentially increases the speed potential of the boat because the vessel will not heel as readily as a monohull. (Plus, there is less surface area and therefore less friction.) As a result, the force of the wind now propels the vessel rather than heels it over.

The drawback to multihulls is that there is typically less storage space than on a monohull. (Multihulls need to remain light to achieve their speeds.) Also, multihulls mean a less conventional layout: on a catamaran, the cockpit and deck area is a flat shallow space between the two hulls; on a trimaran, the space is limited to the slender, centre hull. Multihulls are fast and fun to sail, but to sail them correctly requires specialized knowledge that defies many of the traditional notions of sailing. For this reason, this book describes the sailing of monohulls only.

## Hull materials

There is no right way to build the hull of a sailboat. Whether you choose wood, metal, fibreglass, or even iron-reinforced concrete, the material should be one the limits of which you understand. As with many aspects of boating, the construction of your hull will be influenced by the resources available in your area. Being in close proximity to traditional craftsman – whether in New England, the Pacific Northwest, New Zealand, or Northern Europe – where raw material is still available, might make it feasible to own a wooden boat. Most boatyards today are comfortable working with fibreglass and steel, but it helps to ask around, finding out which yards in your area are capable of what kind of work.

### 1. Wood

The oldest of boatbuilding materials, wood is still used today in many different forms. The traditional style is plank-on-frame: a framework of ribs, which is tied in at the base to the keel and at the top with the deck structure, is then covered in a shell of planks. After being fastened by bronze or steel screws or nails, the planks are caulked in the seams, then primed and painted. Wood does require different care than other hulls. Wood rots for a variety of reasons, including being subjected to poor ventilation (if a cabin is kept closed for long periods, for example); being allowed to sit in fresh water unprotected; or being attacked by marine organisms, such as boring worms.

Other types of wood construction include cold-moulding and strip-planking. Cold-moulded hulls are constructed without heavy frames, but rather, as the name suggests, by using a mould. A series of thin planks, some on diagonals and others running horizontal, are laid across the mould, and epoxy is used to hold the planks together. Cold-moulded hulls are finished more like fibreglass hulls, without being caulked. Many cold-moulded hulls are covered with a layer of glass cloth to ensure protection against moisture before being finished.

Strip-planked hulls are similar in that they are held together by glue and often encased in glass cloth. Strip-plank hulls are made up of narrow strips of wood, stacked one upon another and glued together around a mould to form a shell. The hull is lifted free of the mould when complete and the deck and interior installed.

### 2. Fibreglass (glass-reinforced plastic)

Fibreglass has been in use in boatbuilding for more than 30 years. There are many methods of fibreglass in construction, but, essentially, glass cloth is saturated in liquid glue and then allowed to dry (often being baked or squeezed in a vacuum). This forms an impregnable shell that is impervious to water and strong enough to withstand being pounded by waves and even collisions with other vessels or being grounded.

Depending on what is used as a core – fibreglass is used both inside and out – the hull can be made extremely lightweight and very strong. In the early days of fibreglass, only marine plywood was used. In the intervening years, numerous other structural materials have been used successfully, including balsa wood and a high-tech, honeycomb-like board that is many times lighter than plywood yet still retains stiffness.

Moisture is the enemy of a fibreglass hull. At all costs, a hull needs to be kept free from deep scratches, which can allow moisture to enter the hull's core. Once it creeps in, it is very difficult to get out. A hull with moisture problems is not a total loss, but extensive work is often required: peeling back the layers, then airing out or replacing the affected area, and finally covering and finishing again.

### 3. Steel

Steel is used for its strength and versatility. In construction, it can be bent, twisted, and cut to minute detail. A steel sailboat can be used with confidence while sailing offshore,

## Steering gear

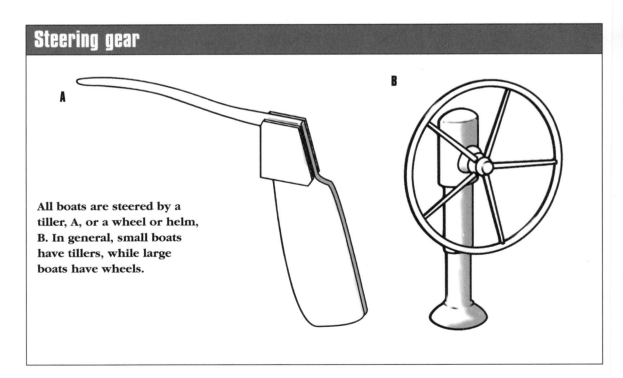

All boats are steered by a tiller, A, or a wheel or helm, B. In general, small boats have tillers, while large boats have wheels.

knowing that a collision – either with another vessel or with a hard, floating object – will not spell certain disaster. The same is true if the vessel grounds, whether on rocks or coral reefs.

The problem with steel, of course, is that it rusts when subjected to moisture. (One naval captain remarked of steel vessels that the only thing they do on their own is rust; everything else takes teamwork.) The owner of a steel sailboat is always seeking ways to prevent moisture from hitting the bare steel and forming rust.

Once rust is established, it can be ground out and a new finish applied, but, if the rust is too extensive, this can lead to serious repair work. However, one benefit of steel is that it is relatively easy to repair using basic welding and cutting skills.

Because of its weight, steel is typically used on large sailboats. It would not make sense to fabricate a 4.25-m (14-ft) steel sailboat, for example, but it might make sense to own a 9-m (30-ft) boat if the owner is comfortable with the material's limits and strength is an important consideration.

## STEERING GEAR

The simplest of steering gear is the tiller. A tiller is a large lever that is attached firmly to the top of the rudder post and used to turn the rudder to port or starboard. Many tillers are equipped with articulated extensions, which enable the helmsman to sit high on the vessel's rail when it is heeling and

## Mast and sails

A rig is made up of the mast(s), A, shrouds and stays, and sails, B.

therefore keep his weight where he wants it and at the same time keep close watch on other vessels and the sails.

Vessels that are equipped with a helm (steering wheel) use a different system to apply turning power to the rudder. The most common style is through use of a cable and quadrant assembly. The helm is connected to a series of cables, which run through a set of sheaves that provide a 'fair lead' back to the rudder post. The cables are then secured to a quadrant, a piece of heavy hardware in the shape of a 90-degree angle (hence the name

## Sailing boat rigging

**Gaff cutter:** A traditional gaff cutter design features two or three headsails (jibs) and the hull is deep, featuring a full keel.

**Schooner:** The schooner rig features two or more masts, the largest of which, the mainmast, is aft.

'quadrant'), which is connected to the rudder post. Cable and quadrant systems are durable; however, because they are hidden from view, they can often be forgotten in routine safety checks.

Another helm design is the traditional worm gear. The helm is fixed to the end of the worm gear, which, when turned in one direction or another, screws a set of arms that are attached to the rudder post. Worm gear assemblies are kept heavily lubricated to minimize friction.

Regardless of what variety of steering assembly is installed on a boat, it is crucial that the system be tight and free of 'play'. Otherwise, dynamic forces are introduced into the system, and these can cause failure in the steering system.

## RIG

The rig of a boat refers to the configuration of a boat's masts and sails. If a vessel is described as a 'sloop' or a 'schooner', the moniker refers to both the number of masts and sails, and where they are positioned in relation to one another. The most common type of rig found today is the simple sloop rig, which comprises a jib and a triangular

**Ketch:** A ketch has the mainmast placed forward of a mizzen mast. A ketch is different from a yawl because it has the mizzen mast forward of the rudder post.

**Sloop:** A simple sloop, the most common rig, includes a mainsail and jib.

**Yawl:** Like a ketch, a yawl has the mainmast forward of a smaller mizzen mast. On a yawl, the mizzen mast is placed abaft the rudder post.

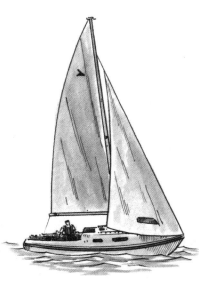

mainsail, also known as a Marconi mainsail – pronounced *mains'l*.

A cutter is a single-masted sailboat the mast of which is stepped a bit further aft than a conventional sloop to make room for the addition of another headsail called a staysail – pronounced *stays'l*.

A ketch is a two-masted sailboat. The after mast, which is the smaller of the two, is called the mizzenmast; and the larger, the mainmast. The sail that flies from the mizzenmast is simply called the mizzen. A ketch can have one, two, or even three headsails.

A yawl looks similar to a ketch. However, a yawl's mizzenmast is typically smaller than that of the ketch and is positioned abaft the boat's rudder post. A ketch's mizzenmast is positioned forward of the rudder post.

A cat rig is a rig without a jib. Most cat boats – not to be confused with catamarans – are single-masted, although one occasionally sees a cat ketch or cat-rigged schooner.

A schooner rig consists of one or more masts, the mainmast being taller (or of equal height) than the foremast. (Large schooners of past centuries carried as many as seven masts.) A typical schooner carries a mainsail aft, rigged either Marconi or gaff (see below);

## Hanging a coil

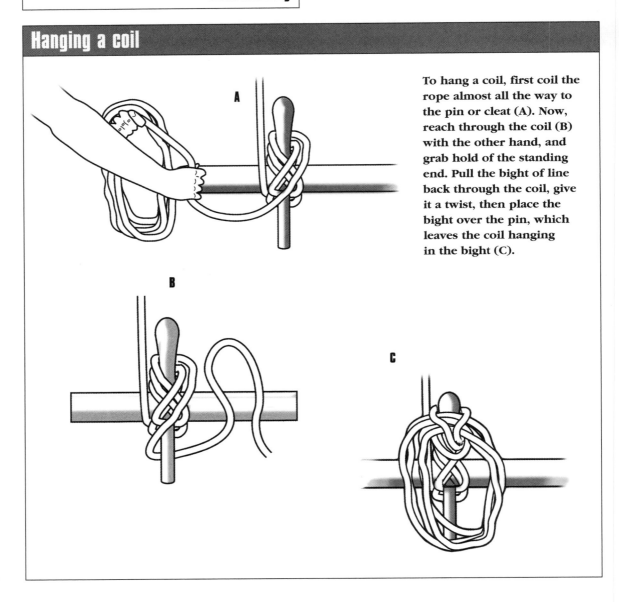

To hang a coil, first coil the rope almost all the way to the pin or cleat (A). Now, reach through the coil (B) with the other hand, and grab hold of the standing end. Pull the bight of line back through the coil, give it a twist, then place the bight over the pin, which leaves the coil hanging in the bight (C).

a gaff foresail or mainstaysail between the two masts; a forestaysail just forward of the foremast; and a jib.

'Gaff-rigged' refers to the shape of a sail. The gaff is the boomlike spar to which the head of the sail is attached. The jaws of the gaff fit around the mast and ride against it when the sail is set.

## RIGGING

### Standing rigging

The standing rigging is the fixed, wire rope that supports the mast, made up of the stays and shrouds.

Shrouds are the wires that hold the mast athwartships, attached to the hull along the sides of the boat through chainplates – heavy-duty hardware that is through-bolted in the hull. Stays support the mast fore and aft, along the centreline. Spreaders are fixed to the mast, typically two-thirds of the way up, and serve to hold the shrouds away from the mast to provide a better angle of support. Most small vessels have single spreaders. (As rigs become taller and more complex, spreaders are added for more support; some megayachts have as many as five or six spreader sets.)

Turnbuckles, also called bottle-screws, enable the adjustment of the tension of stays and shrouds. When setting up the standing rigging for the first time, it is prudent to have experienced assistance on hand. 'Tuning the rig' involves a keen understanding of the loads imposed by the rig on the hull. A rig that is too slack will work itself loose, possibly breaking the mast; a rig that is too tight could cause damage to the hull. The

basic idea of tuning the rig is to have uniform tension throughout the rig, tightened to within the safe working load of the design and the attendant gear.

### Running rigging

Running rigging refers to the soft line of a vessel's rig – in other words, the sheets, halyards, downhauls, and any line connected to the sails, but not a fixed part of the standing rigging.

### DECK

The deck of the boat is the area where the sailor will spend most of his time. It is both the interface between all the forces at work – wind, sails, the water moving past – and the area where the sailor controls, or is subject to, all these forces at work. The deck is where all the lines are handled; where the steering is done; where navigation is carried out; and where a lookout is posted.

Decks are typically constructed of fibreglass, over which a coating of nonskid paint is applied. Along the edges of a deck, at the hull-deck joint, are the bulwarks; on small boats, in particular, these may consist of nothing more than a toerail. Stanchions, which are the vertical supports of lifelines, are secured into the toerail. Holes in the bulwarks or toerail are called the scuppers, which allow water that accumulates on deck (either from falling rain or crashing waves) to drain from the deck.

Like the deck's surface, the tops of any cabins, if they are to be stood upon, are typically coated with nonskid paint. This is especially important on the foredeck, the area of the deck located forward of the mast. The foredeck can often be slippery, because it is the first place to become wet from flying spray. The vessel's anchor is often stowed on the foredeck. Mounted on the foredeck can be a number of cleats or a single post, called a Samson post, for securing dock lines or the anchor rode.

## Belay pin

**Belay pins, used to make off a halyard, were common on older yachts, but they can still be found in use today.**

# A note on direction

- A vessel has a port and starboard side. Why not left and right? If you're facing aft and the helmsman is facing forward, 'left' and 'right' become meaningless. 'Port' and 'starboard' are (like the points of a compass) fixed terms – in other words, 'port' is the side that is on your left only if you are facing forward, 'starboard' the right. There are various ways to remember what each means (for example, the word 'port' has the same number of letters as the word 'left'), but using the terms will lead to familiarity.

- An object located directly off the vessel's side, at an angle of 90 degrees, is considered to be 'off its beam'; a boat's 'beam' is the largest measurement of a vessel's width. In the old days, mariners referred to objects away from the vessel – a lighthouse or another vessel, for example – as being so many 'points' off a vessel's bow, beam, or stern quarters. There are 32 total points around a vessel, divided into sets of four on each side: on the port (or starboard) bow; forward of the port (or starboard) beam; abaft (or aft of) the port (or starboard) beam; and forward of the port (or starboard) quarter. Each of these eight positions has three 'points'. So, for example, a lighthouse that is just off the port bow might be one, two, or three points 'off the port bow.'

- Nowadays, however, at least in the recreational setting, such a system has given way to the use of the clock face for direction. To do this, imagine looking down on the boat and that the deck is positioned on the face of a clock. The bow points towards 12 o'clock; the starboard beam toward three o'clock; the stern towards six o'clock; and the port beam faces nine o'clock. Objects directly forward of the bow are considered 'dead ahead' and directly astern as 'dead astern'.

- When referring to an object in the rig, it is considered to be aloft. A cabin space is referred to as the area belowdecks or down below (as opposed to downstairs). When a vessel is under way, it is considered to be neither tied to a dock nor at anchor (or on a mooring). A vessel aground, according to the Nautical Rules of the Road anyway, is considered under way but not making way, with neither leeway nor steerageway.

- A vessel's course is different from its heading. A heading is the direction the bow is pointing, whether it is at anchor, alongside a dock, or making way. Its course is the direction it is actually moving through the water, affected by its leeway. (A boat can have a course through the water and a course over the ground, often two very different figures if there is current or significant leeway being made.)

- A vessel is subjected to six modes of motion: roll, a side-to-side motion; pitch, a fore-and-aft, hobby-horsing motion; yaw, a screwing motion; heave, a motion that is straight up and down (like a horse on a carousel); sway, a motion that is directly to one side or another on a single plane; and surge, a motion that is directly forward.

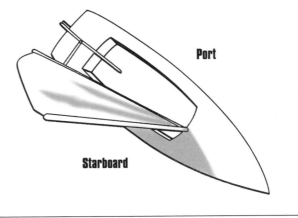

Port

Starboard

## Hatches

Hatches are weathertight doors lying flat on the deck. These can be designed to slide fore and aft or be hinged. Hatches are often equipped with locking mechanisms, which prevent water from entering in even extreme conditions. This is especially important on the foredeck, which will be repeatedly assaulted by boarding waves in rough weather.

## SAILS

Sails are available in several different kinds of fabric, the most common of which is Dacron. Racing boats are nowadays equipped with ever-lighter sails, made from Mylar and Kevlar (the same material used for bulletproof vests). But Dacron remains the dominant fabric for the average sailboat that is not out to win serious races.

Sails are not flat pieces of fabric; they are carefully engineered to be both lightweight and strong. They must resist the force of the wind and the corrosive effects of the sun and marine environment. As a result, sails are typically built by hand and covered with myriad reinforcement patches where the loads will be most concentrated.

A Marconi mainsail and all jibs and staysails have three corners. The top is called the 'head'; the bottom, forward corner (fixed to the mast or to a stay, depending on the sail's use) is the 'tack'; the after, bottom corner is the 'clew'. Note that a gaff sail, being a trapezoid in shape, has two corners at the head; the upper corner is the 'peak' and the lower of the two upper corners is called the 'throat'. The clew and tack remain the same.

As mentioned, sails are not flat; they are built with numerous panels to take the shape of a foil when set and filled with a breeze. This belly shape is called 'roach'.

A sail can be fitted with 'reef points', a series of lines that can be used to reduce the amount of sail area if the wind blows hard. When a sail is reefed, a new clew and tack are formed by using the 'reef outhaul' and spare lashing line. Reef points are used to tie the spare sail along the foot, around the sail's 'boltrope'. (For more detail, *see* Chapter 7.)

## Halyards

A halyard is a line that raises a sail. One end of the halyard is attached to the head of the sail, and the other is made off at the base of the mast. In between, the halyard goes up the mast, through a sheave, and back down again. A

**Mainsheet**

The mainsheet controls the trim of the mainsail, typically set up to offer a degree of mechanical advantage to the operator seated in the cockpit.

halyard can be put to a winch for more hauling power or can be run through a series of several blocks (known as pulleys).

Most halyards today are made of soft rope, although there are still some wire halyards around. Wire was used for halyards to varying degrees of success for many years; the benefit is that steel does not stretch, the drawback is that it is a nuisance to handle. Specialized sheaves and winches were needed for wire. Today, halyards are typically made of either twisted or laid Dacron, a man-made fibre that has little stretch and is exceedingly strong.

### Sheets

The lines that control the angle – or trim – of sails are known as the sheets. (The sheets are not the sails themselves, a common mistake.) Sheets are secured to the foot of the sail – either to a boom, if so equipped, or to the clew of the sail directly.

## Halyard

A halyard passes through a sheave at the top of the mast, then comes down to be handled on deck.

## Windlass

An anchor windlass gives extra pulling power to the foredeck crew for recovering the anchor. Windlasses can be mechanical, electric, or hydraulic.

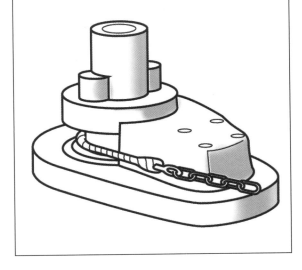

### Topping lift

It is sometimes convenient to have the boom supported when the sail is not set. An adjustable line that runs from the masthead to the end of the boom is called a topping lift. It can be used to raise the boom safely over one's head or lowered into the boom crutch or gallows. A topping lift can also be used to give extra shape to a sail when wind is light.

### Downhaul

Secured to the sail's tack, a downhaul secures the sail to the boat so that the halyard can be hauled tight. Without the downhaul being secure, the tack of the sail will be loose and the luff of the sail not snug against the mast.

### Vang

Particularly when sailing on a reach or a run, booms can be forced upwards by the motion of the wind. This can ruin the foil shape. A vang, typically a series of blocks with an adjustable line or a hydraulic ram on larger boats, keeps the end of the boom in position.

## BLOCKS

Blocks can be used for a variety of purposes aboard a small sailing vessel. A block consists of a sheave (pronounced *shiv*), which turns effortlessly around a pin with the aid of bearings. Bearings can be made of steel, lubed with a heavy grease, or of high-tech plastics such as Kevlar. Cheeks of the block hold the assembly together. Blocks can be used to provide a better lead for a line, to avoid an obstruction, or to run the line to a more convenient location for handling; or, when used together to form a block-and-tackle assembly, to increase pulling power; or for all of the above together. A mainsheet assembly is a good example of a system that is meant to be set up in a convenient way, both out of the way but easy to access, and at the same time offer the crew the advantage of not needing to apply a great deal of force to trim the sail.

A single block offers no advantage in pulling power. A double-block assembly offers two-to-one power, minus the friction of the sheaves themselves. A three-block system offers three-to-one power, and so on.

## CLEATS

A cleat is a two-horned piece of equipment, typically made of bronze or stainless steel, around which line is tied. Cleats are typically through-bolted to the deck, reinforced with strong backing plates that will not tear out when a load is imposed.

## SNATCH-BLOCK

A snatch block is like a portable block. The top of the block can be unlocked and the sheave exposed, allowing a line to be slipped into the block without needing to pass the bitter end through the sheave. This is a handy function when you need to capture a line

that is already set up somewhere, perhaps re-leading a jib sheet so that it will not foul on hardware or chafe against another sail.

## WINCHES

A winch is like a portable block and tackle. It enables a sailor to apply significant power to a line when necessary – for example, hauling up a sail with a halyard or trimming the sheets. Winches are a series of gears, which reduce the load on the line to a load that is easily handled by a single person wielding a winch handle. Winches can be mounted flat on deck, as with a sheet winch; or sideways

---

### Constructing a handy-billy

One of the more useful tools in a boat's locker, the handy-billy is like a portable crew member. A handy-billy enables a single person to handle great loads for a variety of reasons, whether hauling up a fouled anchor or tightening the rig.

A handy-billy consists of two double blocks and a length of line. Each of the blocks should be equipped with a hook on the top and a becket – a steel tab for shackling in one end of the line – on the bottom. The diameter of the line and the size of the sheaves will be determined by the intended loads.

Most small boats would be well served by having a handy-billy constructed of 1-cm (1/2-in) line. The rope should be approximately 15–18m (50–60ft) long and be whipped at one end. Splice the other end around a thimble of the same diameter as the line, then secure this splice to the becket of one of the blocks.

Then reeve the line through one of the sheaves of the other block and continue as in the illustration. A handy-billy can deliver enormous loads; remember to use it with extreme caution.

## Oars versus engine

When the wind is not blowing, or if it is blowing from the wrong direction and a person has tired of working to windward, there comes a time when a sailor reaches for alternative power to propel his or her boat. Many small sailing vessels are equipped with outboard motors, affixed to the sterns by brackets. Other vessels can be rigged with oarlocks and propelled by rowing power, provided the vessel is small enough and the backs doing the rowing strong enough.

The advantage of an inboard or outboard motor is obvious: when you want to move the boat effortlessly, you start the engine, engage the gear, and throttle up. The drawback is the maintenance that these mechanical devices require to ensure operational reliability. Too often, sailors ignore their outboard motors, yet by having them either strapped to the stern or inboard, they come to rely on their being able to start when needed. Maintenance includes regular oil changes for four-stroke and diesel engines; frequent cleaning with fresh water; the changing of sacrificial zinc anodes; and attention to plugs, filters, and pumps. If neglected, your maintenance schedule will be guaranteed to haunt you when you least expect. The engine is a simple machine with simple requirements, but it needs regular attention.

If, on the other hand, an outboard or inboard engine represents an aspect of boating you could do without, consider having your boat propelled by oars. This will make you a better sailor, as you'll be more inclined to use the wind for every last movement of the boat, knowing that without the sails it will be your arms and back that will need to move the boat's mass.

When considering whether oars are possible on your boat, take into account the boat's beam – in other words, the distance from one side to the other, where the oarlocks would be positioned: you will want to have oars long enough to reach the water at a reasonable angle. Also, consider where to store them. Most of all, however, consider the overall weight of the vessel.

on a mast, as for use with a halyard. Always remove a winch handle from a winch, stowing it in a pouch or locker, to prevent it being accidentally lost overboard. It is sometimes helpful to have two people operate a winch, one person to crank the handle and the other to 'tail' – that is, take up the line that is gained by the winch going around. (Always wrap line round a winch clockwise; it will not work otherwise.) After taking three wraps around the winch and tightening the winch to the desired tension, take the line to a cleat and make off the line. Winches can also be equipped to be self-tailing, utilizing an extra, grooved sheave mounted atop the winch that captures the line and maintains tension.

## Cleat

A cleat is a basic piece of deck hardware and, depending on placement, can be used to make off sheets, halyards, dock lines, or running backstays.

## COCKPIT

The cockpit is the large seating area in the stern where the helmsman sits to steer the vessel. Many times, all the lines are led into the cockpit to facilitate handling of the sails and to allow the crew to stay off the slippery foredeck. On smaller boats, the cockpit is shallow with room only for one's feet.

A comfortable cockpit can define how enjoyable a boat is to sail. A small, awkward cockpit will cramp the crew. A large, comfortable cockpit with an ergonomic design makes a boat a thrill to sail. Is there a place to brace one's feet? Is there a backrest? Will the boom hit you square in the nose if you are sitting upright, or is it high enough to clear even a tall person's head? These details have very real meaning in the marine environment.

A cockpit is often equipped with storage lockers on either side, which can be used to stow winch handles, fenders, spare line, navigation equipment, and signalling devices.

The bottom of the cockpit is called the sole, not the floor. The cockpit is equipped with scuppers so that any water that enters the cockpit can be drained over the side.

## BELOWDECKS

In a small daysailer, the belowdecks area is often nothing more than a small cuddy cabin, a covered space that is used for storage and barely large enough for a person to get out of the elements. A larger sailboat will have a cabin that is accessed by a companionway, typically covered by a sliding hatch and a series of washboards – small pieces of wood that can be slid into the small opening leading below. A companionway ladder leads below.

## SEACOCKS

If equipped with an inboard engine or a marine toilet, or any system that requires saltwater for use, a boat will be equipped with seacocks. A seacock is a bronze valve, typically a ball valve, which allows seawater to enter through the hull.

Seacocks are used for the intake of raw seawater for an inboard engine or for use in a marine toilet. Seacocks are also used to discharge the waste water from the boat. As with any system, seacocks need maintenance. Inspection and lubrication of the valve should be performed regularly.

# CHAPTER 3

# Essential sailing equipment

**The amount and variety of gear aboard your boat will vary with the size of the boat, its intended use, and the type of person you are.**

If you are a 'gear head', you will probably want to equip your boat with the latest in navigational gadgetry, to line the rails with complicated safety gear to be on hand in response to any type of emergency, and to fill your lockers with spares and just-in-case tools. However, having too much gear, especially if it is never used and its purpose is little understood, can be as dangerous as having too little. Indeed, it is likely to imbue the crew with a false sense of security. So, if you have the gear on your boat, learn how to use it. On the other hand, if you're a minimalist, be certain that you have thought through your simple-is-better approach. You should not refrain from purchasing certain basic safety equipment if it is essential.

This chapter will list the myriad gear available to sailors for equipping a boat for service on the sea or other waterways. It is not intended to be a complete list of what every boat should carry. Each skipper has to decide what is appropriate for her boat, considering the customs of the area, the laws, and especially the specific hazards that may exist. Environmental conditions may include cold water, strong prevailing winds, or large ocean swells. A boat's specific list of safety concerns might include the extent of its freeboard (the distance from the water to the deck), which may make it difficult for a crew member to climb aboard from the water unassisted; a

low boom, which could hit an unsuspecting crew member in the forehead even if he is seated; and a cramped cockpit, which might make it difficult for crew members to safely handle sails during manoeuvres.

When equipping boats for sea, bear in mind that simpler is probably better. Take the time to understand each piece of equipment, using the gear during benign conditions or even on shore, if possible. It is possible to misuse even something as simple as a hand-held pump. This has a long plastic cylinder

## Binoculars

Scanning the horizon and the waters close to your boat should be done frequently. The law requires that you keep a lookout posted at all times.

## Charting a course

Plotting tools, such as parallel rules and dividers, take some time to master, but are essential devices for safe navigation. Take the time to learn how to use them properly.

that houses the valve and a flexible hose that discharges the water, and, during an emergency, panic might mean that you insert the wrong end overboard, resulting in water being pumped into the boat.

Think of your boat as a reflection of who you are as a person, and equip your boat to reflect this fact. So, if you're more comfortable with mechanical objects, don't frustrate yourself with excessive electronic gear. Remember, too, that the more electrical systems you have, the more you need to be aware of their functions and limits. Keep your

gear, and your boat as a whole, within your personal limits. If the limits of the equipment exceed your knowledge or abilities, leave it on the dock. Or, if the equipment is essential, learn more about how to use it before you leave the dock.

### SAFETY GEAR

There are two categories of safety gear: personal gear and gear for the boat. Personal gear is equipment that is intended to maintain the health and safety of crew members (life jackets, recovery gear for a

## Types of life jacket

A. A child's life jacket should be equipped with a crotch strap and fit snugly. Otherwise, a child can easily slip out of the device when immersed in water, rendering it useless.

B. A Type I life jacket is designed to keep an unconscious person upright, head above water, but it is too cumbersome to wear regularly and should only be worn in emergencies.

C. Many life jackets are designed for safety and comfort, and can be worn on a boat at all times.

**B**

**A**

**C**

man overboard); and safety gear for the boat includes objects that will protect the boat from certain distress, such as pumps, fire extinguishers, and emergency patch kits.

Most countries (including Britain and the United States) require that you have certain minimal safety gear for the type of boat you operate – this means, but is not limited to, having enough life jackets for everyone on board. It is a good idea to wear a life jacket at all times when you are on or around a small boat, and in many countries this is a legal necessity for children. You can purchase slim life jackets, or even inflatable-harness life jackets, that are designed to allow the wearer the necessary flexibility for moving about a small boat with ease.

## Life jackets

The Safety of Life At Sea (SOLAS) Treaty, which is upheld by the International Maritime Organization and endorsed by the world's coastguards, divides life jackets into categories: Type I to Type III are wearable, and Types IV and V are throwable devices.

- Type I life jackets are large, blocklike, and awkward to wear around a boat. They are intended to maintain an unconscious person in the water in an upright position so that his airway is unobstructed.
- Type II life jackets offer somewhat less buoyancy, and are still fairly awkward, but are not intended to keep an unconscious person upright.
- Type III life jackets are more comfortable to wear. Although not intended to keep an unconscious person upright in the water, they do offer good overall flotation and full freedom of motion, making them easy to wear at all times.

Each country has slightly different laws on the subject, but you should know what the limit of each life jacket is and equip your vessel accordingly. Life jackets should fit snugly. Children should have life jackets that are intended to be worn by children: each year, numerous children are drowned as a result of slipping out of life jackets that are intended to be worn by a larger person. Even if you choose not to wear a life jacket at all times, be sure that you have tried them on and know how all the straps are intended to be secured.

Wearing a life jacket is a good idea even for people who consider themselves strong swimmers. If you are knocked overboard, this usually comes as a surprise: you might be hit on the head by the boom or pushed off the slippery foredeck by a flapping jib sheet; you will probably be fully clothed when you enter the water, possibly wearing shoes; you may be injured – unconscious even – by whatever knocked you in; you may have entered the water at an awkward angle, perhaps on your back; and you might be struck by the boat's hull as it continues to move through the waves. The perceived burden of wearing a life jacket is minor compared to what it can do to save your life. And floating on the surface, instead of gasping for breath and using all your strength to stay afloat, will mean that you can help your crew to bring you back aboard – an operation that will be fraught with enough hazard and confusion in the best of circumstances.

Keep in mind that the law represents only a minimum standard of safety. If you do not choose to wear a Type I life jacket at all times and the law requires that you have one on board for each crew member, you may choose to stow these Type I life jackets and have crew members wear a set of Type III.

Inflatable life jackets are commonly used on small sailboats for crew who want good buoyancy protection, but do not want to limit their range of motion. Inflatable life jackets are equipped with $CO_2$ cartridges that inflate a set of airbags when a dissolvable seal is immersed in water. In the United

States, the Coast Guard has approved certain inflatable life jackets as Type I, and these, when fully inflated, will maintain an unconscious person upright in the water. Be sure to inspect the expiration dates on your inflatable life jackets. Also, take care not to get them wet when cleaning or stowing them after use. They will inflate if immersed in water and you will have to install a new cartridge. Many inflatable life jackets are fitted with safety harnesses.

## SAFETY HARNESS

A safety harness should be standard equipment, one for each crew member, on any boat that sails offshore – whether on overnight excursions or long daysails. It should be worn at all times during rough weather: if a boat heels suddenly, if green water sweeps over the deck, an unsuspecting crew member can be swept over the side in an instant.

A safety harness has two components: the chest harness and the tether. The tether (often two lengths of webbing and a pair of clips) is clipped or hitched to the harness through a set of stainless steel D-rings. (For some reason, these two pieces of equipment are typically sold separately in marine supply stores.) Harnesses and tethers are constructed of heavy-duty nylon webbing with reinforced stitching. When purchasing, look for a label indicating that the item has been approved by the country's governing agency. Also note that some tethers are constructed of heavy-duty elastic webbing, which reduces the length of line when not in use and also helps to absorb some of the shock when the line suddenly comes tight.

The best place to clip a tether to the boat is in a position along the centreline. This gives the crew member a range of motion that includes both sides of the vessel. A line that is rigged specifically to allow harnesses be clipped to it is called a jackline. A jackline should run the length of the deck along the centreline, allowing crew to move to the foredeck to handle sails without unclipping.

It may be necessary to rig one jackline on each side of the boat. Whenever transferring a tether from one jackline to another point, transfer one tether at a time. That way, you remain clipped to the boat by at least one tether at all times. (The same is true when working aloft.) If you are expecting to remain in a single position for a long period – in the cockpit, for example – it is prudent to clip directly into a padeye.

While it may not be appropriate to have a jackline rigged at all times, take the time to consider when the line can be rigged if you plan on sailing away from shore or in extreme conditions. Practise rigging a jackline and clipping into it. If the skipper determines that a jackline is to be rigged, every member of the crew should be secured to the line while on deck.

When is it time to don a safety harness? If you have chosen to purchase inflatable life jackets with integral harness and tether, your choice is made for you: you are always wearing both a life jacket and harness. If not, your judgement of the conditions, the abilities of the crew, and the nature of the sailing – even the tack your boat is on – will determine when it is time to clip in.

## PERSONAL SAFETY GEAR
### Lights

Each crew member should have a personal, waterproof light clipped to his harness. In the event of a man overboard at night, this light can be turned on by the person in the water. There are several styles of lights, ranging in sophistication from the chemically powered glow sticks that are cracked open in emergencies, to those that are battery powered and can direct a single, powerful, focused beam of light or a pulsing strobe light.

Whichever is chosen, be sure to check at the start of each sailing season that the lights

## Throwable devices

A person who falls into the water should be recovered immediately. A life ring tossed immediately after the person goes in the water can save that person's life.

and batteries are being used within the expiration date printed on the products.

### Whistles

Personal whistles are also helpful. Compact safety whistles that are fitted with taglines can be hitched or tied to a safety harness or life jacket and remain out of the way during sailing, yet still be within reach during an emergency. Not only are whistles handy during man-overboard emergencies – particularly in the dark or in heavy weather – but they also can be used to alert other vessels, or those on shore, to an emergency. Crew members should be instructed that whistles are to be sounded only during an actual emergency.

### Personal signalling devices

More complex personal safety gear is available for the ambitious sailor, including radio-powered man-overboard devices. These systems use water-activated transmitters, clipped to each person's harness, to sound an alarm that is wired into the boat, alerting other crew that a person has gone over the side. Some personal signalling devices are even fitted with long-range portable transmitters, which can alert passing airplanes of an overboard person's position.

### THROWABLE DEVICES

When a crew member goes into the water, the cry of 'Man overboard!' should be announced immediately. Within seconds, a life ring should be thrown towards the person in the water.

Life rings should be painted with the boat's name and hailing port. These vary in construction. The most basic is the ring buoy, which should be equipped with a length of line (polypropylene is a good choice because it floats). When the ring is thrown, one end of the line should remain on deck.

On larger vessels, it is helpful to secure an MOB (man overboard) pole to the ring on a length of line. MOB poles are weighted on one end, with a foam buoy for a base, and have a flag at the other. When tossed into the water, the pole will stand up in the waves, indicating to the person in the water the exact location of the ring – and to the crew left aboard the boat, the likely location of the person in the water. Seeing a person's head bobbing in the waves is nearly impossible in all but the calmest conditions.

All MOB gear should be secured in the cockpit in such a way that it will not be knocked loose accidentally, but remain easily accessible and deployable at all times.

If a person needs to go into the water, either to clear a fouled propeller or to go for a swim, consider using a throw bag. Such devices, which include a length of polypropylene line stuffed into a buoyant nylon bag, can be clipped to the rail and thrown over the side. The bag will stream astern of a vessel that is under way or float downwind or downcurrent if the vessel is at anchor.

### Life sling

A life sling combines the versatility of a throwable ring with a means of bringing this person back aboard safely and easily. Horseshoe-shaped, a life sling is thrown to a person in the water, who then climbs into the device so that the flotation is around his shoulders. Meanwhile, the vessel is brought to a stop, either by striking sail or heading into the wind. The person can be hauled back to the vessel, clipped in close to the hull, then the line put to a winch. That way, the person, who may be weak with the effects of fatigue and fear, can be recovered with significant mechanical advantage. In any case, she may even be incapable of climbing a ladder or helping herself aboard.

### LADDERS

A ladder is both a safety item and an enjoyable addition to a boat's gear locker. Some ladders can be of hard construction, such as stainless steel or wood; or soft, built of line that incorporates rigid treads. Any ladder, whether soft or rigid, should be secured to the vessel's toerail or lifelines, and extend down the side of the hull into the water. A ladder that includes a step or two below the waterline is especially helpful, as it enables the person in the water – either someone who has fallen overboard accidentally or is simply taking a swim – to use his legs as well as his arms to lift his weight.

Ladders built of rope are not only easy to make, but also handy. First, they can be stowed easily, rolled up and placed in a deck locker; and secondly, they do not bang against the hull. Rope ladders should have two attachment points. A rope ladder with a single attachment point will swing when a person steps on a rung, turning the act of climbing back aboard into an exhausting gymnastic experience.

Rigid ladders need to be used with care, and require a perfect, and in some cases custom, fit; otherwise, they will come loose at the worst possible moment. If a rigid ladder rests against the hull, be sure that the points protruding towards the hull are capped in rubber, to ensure good grip against the smooth hull and prevent chafe or scratching. Many rigid ladders can be folded up and secured in place to the vessel's lifelines. This feature saves precious stowage space.

If using a ladder for getting back aboard a vessel from a smaller vessel such as an inflatable tender or dinghy, be sure to deploy adequate fenders on each side of the ladder, forward and aft, regardless of whether the ladder is soft or rigid. Further, be sure that the fenders are of the correct diameter to ensure that they will provide ample cushion when the weight of another vessel comes against them.

## LIFE RAFTS

There are several different types of life raft available for small sailboats. Many people consider their dinghy to be their life raft, especially if it is the inflatable variety that will continue to maintain its positive buoyancy even if filled with water.

How far to venture from land is a matter of judgement and means taking into account many environmental conditions such as cold water and rough seas, but any vessel that ventures far should have some alternate means of keeping a person afloat and removed from complete immersion in the water. A life jacket will keep a person afloat, but bear in mind that the insidious effects of hypothermia will overwhelm a person immersed in water for long periods of time. Even relatively warm water, say 24°–29°C (75°–85°F), will eventually draw warmth from a person's body and cause hypothermia.

Many sailboats are equipped with inflatable life rafts that, when manually

## The boarding ladder

A boarding ladder is as much a safety device as it is a useful piece of gear for swimming. A proper boarding ladder should extend below the water's surface for ease of use.

deployed or immersed in water, are instantly inflated. These rafts, which are mandatory on certain large commercial vessels and small passenger vessels that transit open ocean, allow the victim to climb completely out of the water. Some inflatable life rafts are equipped with a canopy, which shelters the

# Life raft

Every vessel that ventures offshore or on extended passages should be equipped with a life raft for use as a last resort in an emergency.

victims from exposure to the elements, whether rain or sun. Life rafts are ringed in safety lines, so that a person in the water can cling to the sides of the raft until finding a way to climb inside. Be sure to secure an inflatable life raft in such a way that the hydrostatic release, which is water-activated, will effectively free the raft from the vessel in distress.

If conditions are extreme – strong winds or breaking seas – life rafts can be prematurely forced away from the vessel, or they can be capsized. For this reason, many rafts are equipped with a fabric ballasting system, a sack that hangs beneath the raft platform and acts as a sea anchor, creating drag that slows the momentum of the raft as it is tossed by the waves and buffeted by the wind.

Whether you choose a raft with a canopy or ballasting system – or whether you choose to use an inflatable raft at all – should be determined by the prevailing conditions and

54

the type of sailing you are expecting to do. Cold water should certainly influence your decision, as should any planned offshore passages. If an offshore passage is in the offing, but most of your sailing is done close to land, consider renting an inflatable raft. Many chandleries and safety organizations (and yacht clubs) rent rafts by the week or by the month.

### Life float

Another option is the life float. Constructed of closed-cell foam, a life float is stored on deck and is more cumbersome than the inflatable raft, yet does not have any moving parts and is therefore practically maintenance-free. An inflatable life raft can be stowed in a small space and hold a large number of people, whereas a closed-cell life float cannot be reduced in size – what you see is what you get. Always inspect life floats to ensure that the safety lines, which ring the float, are in good condition. Remember, the effects of the sun can quickly degrade any equipment that is not covered.

Some floats are equipped with netting in the middle, which is intended to cradle people at the water's surface. While the netting will not keep people from getting wet, it allows victims to be mostly removed from the water. Life floats should clearly indicate the number of people they are intended to support.

### SOUND SIGNALS

A sound signal is any device intended to signal another vessel. According to the Rules of the Road, there are numerous instances when vessels should make certain sound signals – in restricted visibility, when manoeuvring in close proximity to other vessels, or when leaving a berth.

A sound signal can be as simple as a lung-powered horn fitted with a vibrating valve that makes a sound like an aggressive goose. While sounding somewhat ridiculous, these signals can be heard over long distances and

## Fenders

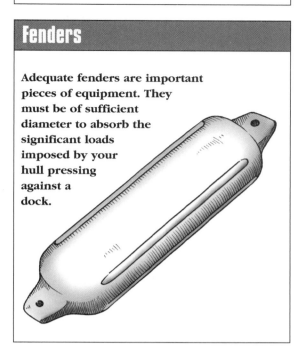

Adequate fenders are important pieces of equipment. They must be of sufficient diameter to absorb the significant loads imposed by your hull pressing against a dock.

are especially valuable on board a small boat that may need to make a large noise. These devices have no moving parts and are the best choice where simplicity is desired. However, they are built of metal and will therefore rust if left exposed to the elements over long periods, so store them in a cockpit locker for quick access. Keep in mind that, while these devices sound loud to you, even when blown softly, you may be trying to attract the attention of a large, powered vessel, whose operator may not be listening for such a noise or whose hearing may be muffled by the noise of his engine. When you need to use these devices, blow loud, crisp signals – as prescribed by the Rules.

Handheld air-powered horns are also a useful piece of equipment. The plastic top is fitted with a valve – activated by a single button or trigger – that forces air through the small horn. Although diminutive in size, the horns are capable of shrill blasts. There is no mistaking the distinctive noise of a high-pitched air horn. Such a horn may be preferable over the lung-powered one in a busy commercial harbour. Be aware that the amount of gas within the canister will eventually be used up. It is prudent to have a spare canister on board.

## FLARES

Flares are flammable devices that can be held in the hand or fired from a pistol. When ignited, flares emit a powerful, bright flame that is visible for miles. Flares can be exceedingly useful during emergency situations, as they can assist rescue workers, either in aircraft or surface vessels, to locate your vessel and crew.

Extra care should be taken to keep flares, and their related equipment, in dry storage areas. Do not stow flares loose in a cockpit locker; they will become wet and be useless in an emergency. It is best to store them in a waterproof box in a location that is secure but easily accessible in an emergency. If you have equipped your vessel with an abandon ship bag (see below), store the flares in the same location as this bag.

Flares are extremely dangerous. They can inflict harmful – even fatal – wounds if used improperly. If you have a flare gun, always remember that these devices are intended to be shot directly into the air – and not in the direction of whomever is coming to your aid. Also, shooting a flare straight up will indicate your presence more precisely – and illuminate your vessel – than if you fire it at an angle.

Flares are marked with expiration dates. Heed all warnings and restrictions printed on the labels; they are there for your protection after all.

## Signalling devices

Sound signals can be powered by compressed air, such as the one pictured, or by lung power. Be sure that your equipment is in working order.

## EPIRBS

An emergency positioning indicating radio beacon (EPIRB) is intended to be activated only in an absolute emergency, when the vessel is in certain jeopardy. When activated, either manually or by immersion in water, a radio signal is emitted from the device and transmitted to a satellite, and then to a shore-based rescue station. Most EPIRBs today transmit coded emergency signals at 406 MHz. (Older 121.5 MHz EPIRBs, although still available for purchase, are less accurate and do not send out a signal that identifies the vessel.) The 406 EPIRB is designed to float and can be activated automatically or by flipping a switch. The EPIRB should be mounted in a

# Getting help

Each vessel should be equipped with emergency equipment that is designed to communicate distress.

A variety of gear is available, from the smoke (A) and flare signals (C) to the VHF radio (B) or cell phone. Even a signal mirror (D) can be used in certain emergencies.

cabin space or other protected area and taken with the crew if you are forced to abandon ship.

When you purchase a 406 MHz EPIRB, you will fill out a form that identifies your vessel and includes a space for emergency contact information. It is imperative that this information be kept up to date. Rescue by public organizations are complicated and costly, and risk the lives of numerous individuals who will respond to your distress signal by surface vessel or aircraft, or both. The decision to activate an EPIRB is not to be taken lightly and must be considered a last resort, to be used only for saving lives (not property).

## WINCH HANDLES

Winch handles are an essential piece of equipment for operating deck winches. Always remove the handle from the winch after working the line and stow the handle in its proper place. This might be a specified locker or a tightly fitting sleeve mounted to the mast or a cabin trunk. You don't want your winch handle to slip overboard, which it will do if left on deck or if the storage space is less than secure. Consider purchasing a spare winch handle.

## SPARES KIT

Every boat should carry certain spare parts. But you don't need to jam your storage lockers so full of spares and speciality tools that you could perform large-scale rebuilds or industrial salvage jobs. So what should be in the kit?

- Take note of the removable objects on your boat – the shackles, rope, clevis and cotter pins, D-rings – and consider having a few extras on board.
- Take an inventory if the boat is new to you, removing any object that has no obvious need. Over the course of a boat's lifetime, previous owners may have loaded all their useless junk into the lockers, thinking it might one day come in handy.

- Carry spare fuses for each device connected to the electrical system, including VHF radio, GPS unit, or freshwater pump.
- Carry a roll of duct tape and a roll of electrical or rigging tape for chafe protection or line repairs. Scraps of canvas or Dacron also help to combat chafe.
- Several coils of line, which are of the same diameter as your running rigging, should also be aboard.
- A set of small nuts and bolts and different-sized wood screws will come in handy for any number of repairs.
- Hose clamps – be sure to have all sizes necessary – can secure hoses, and wire ties can prevent chafe and keep wires out of the way.
- Your engine's systems might need lubrication. Consider carrying samples of grease and lubricating oil that apply to your vessel's systems. Through-hull fittings should be overhauled with heavy waterproof grease. A steering system's worm gear requires similar treatment. If the vessel is equipped with a marine toilet, a daily application of cooking oil will keep the valves supple. Winches need to be dosed regularly with light-duty oil. (Note that spray oil tends to make things sticky over time and should be avoided on a boat.)
- Each through-hull fitting should have a wooden plug tied to it for use in case of failure. (If the valve becomes stuck open and the hose is leaking water, jam the plug into the through hull.) Always carry spare plugs of various sizes. Plugs can also be used to temporarily stop the end of a coolant, water, or fuel hose while affecting repairs.

## ENGINE SPARES

If your vessel is equipped with an inboard diesel engine, you will be well advised to carry a few spares. Such a list could include several different-sized coolant hoses, spare belts, engine zincs, pump impellers, and spare fuel filters. Your engine's manual should list a complete spares kit in the appendix, giving the size and model number of each part.

The single most important maintenance task you can do to extend the life of your engine is to change the oil and filters (both fuel and lubricating oil) regularly. Your engine manual will describe how frequently this should be done. At the very least, though, you should ensure that it is done once per season. (See the section on Engine Care in the chapter Getting Started.)

## TOOL KIT

Every vessel should have a basic tool kit: wrenches; basic socket set; pliers; hammer; rubber mallet; a screwdriver set; alan and hex key set; wire-crimping tool; razor knife; and channel-lock pliers. Mark your tools with your boat's name in permanent marker; this will save you wondering about a tool's ownership in a busy boatyard – especially if you hire outside assistance from a rigger or mechanic who might bring his own set of tools onto your boat.

If your vessel has an engine, be sure to have a set of wrenches that are large enough to handle the nut that secures the stuffing box. (The stuffing box is the through-hull fitting through which the propeller shaft passes; the nut tightens around the shaft to minimize the flow of water, which is intended to keep the fitting from becoming overheated due to friction.)

Always keep your tools stored in a dry location, and keep them well oiled. Consider keeping an oiled cloth in the toolbox, covering the tools when they are stored. Use the cloth to wipe them down after use. Even if your tools do not become wet, they will rust because of the salty, moist air.

## Abandon ship kit

A. Sea anchor
B. Paddles
C. First-aid kit
D. Fishing line
E. Bellows
F. Quoit and line
G. Survival leaflets
H. Bailer

I. Repair kit, flares, sponge, knife
J. Water, can openers, sea sickness pills
K. Torch
L. Resealing lids

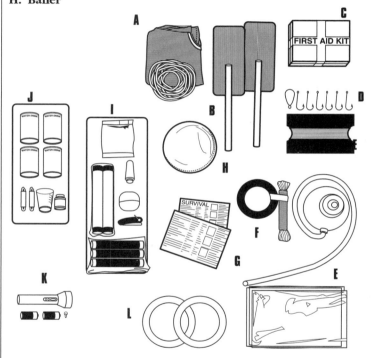

## Abandoning ship

Abandoning a vessel for a life raft should be seen as a last resort. Do not abandon your vessel unless you are absolutely certain that it is unsafe, either sinking rapidly or experiencing an uncontrollable fire, for example. Many vessels will remain afloat even when completely swamped with the aid of reserve buoyancy.

Each vessel should have an abandon ship bag for use in an emergency. The bag should be grabbed just prior to abandoning your vessel. When considering what to include, think about the type of sailing you will do and the geographic conditions, including water temperature and climate.

If you can, take your VHF radio with you – as a lifeline to the outside world, this may prove to be the most important piece of equipment.

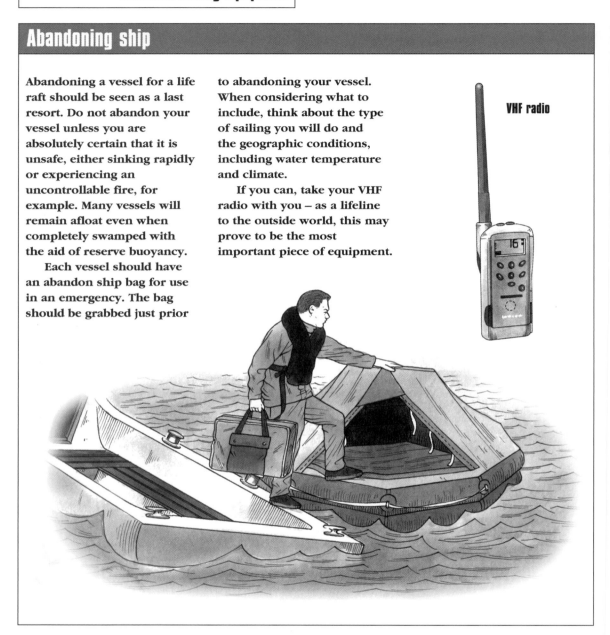

VHF radio

### ABANDON SHIP KIT

An abandon ship bag should be small, packed in such a way that, if fully immersed, it will remain waterproof. It should be stowed in a prominent location, and it should be taken with you whenever you are considering abandoning your vessel – whether due to grounding, sinking, fire, or any other emergency that means the certain loss of your boat. Abandon your vessel only when it is clear that it is lost and nothing more can be done to save it. Even staying with a capsized vessel is likely to be far preferable to clinging to a small, open raft. Furthermore, a sailboat in distress is easier to spot than a drifting raft.

An abandon ship bag should reflect the type of sailing you do. If you are planning offshore passages, the bag should include far more supplies, such as survival gear, than a bag that is stored aboard your daysailer that you use for cruising the coast.

Remember, an abandon ship bag should be waterproof and should be positively buoyant, even when fully loaded.

Consider the following items for use in a basic abandon ship bag:

- A handheld VHF radio, either waterproof or packed in a waterproof case, will enable you to speak with a rescue agency or private vessel crew. Remember that a VHF provides only line-of-sight communications. (Only vessels and stations that are within a few miles of each other can communicate via VHF.)
- Hypothermia blankets – specialized polyurethane sheets – maintain a person's warmth in emergencies and are important as hypothermia causes confusion and can all too easily prove fatal.
- A water bottle – kept almost full – should be in every such kit to combat dehydration. Consider changing the water, or purchasing canned water, regularly to keep it fresh.
- Nutritious snacks which can withstand long-term storage maintain a person's energy level at a point where rational decisions can still be made. A person who is dehydrated and hungry is likely to make poor decisions and thus contribute to the confusion.
- Signal mirrors, equipped with a small hole in the centre for aiming the beam, are excellent, low-tech emergency devices.

- A handheld compass will assist in keeping track of your position in relation to other objects and enable you to communicate more educated directions to rescue personnel.
- A basic survival kit could prove useful. Be sure to include fish hooks, a knife, wire, small twine, waterproof matches and a cigarette lighter, and a small pair of pliers.
- A first-aid kit, but remember that this should be stored separately from the abandon ship bag as it will probably be used frequently for superficial injuries throughout the boating season, for bandages, seasickness medication, or antiseptic cream.

## FIRST-AID KIT

Every boat should have a first-aid kit, packed with supplies that the skipper knows how to use for the treatment of superficial wounds and illnesses. Include:

- Anti-bacterial soap, for flushing open wounds. Personal cleanliness aboard a boat is crucial; it helps prevent infection and speeds recovery.
- A handbook that discusses first-aid treatment specifically as it pertains to the marine environment.
- Seasickness medication, which can alleviate certain mild effects of this insidious affliction.
- A package of assorted sterile bandages.
- Antiseptic ointment.
- Epinephrine kit for food and animal sting allergies, especially if you host guests whose particular health issues you may not know. Antihistamines alleviate the minor effects of food and animal sting reactions, called anaphylactic emergencies.
- Sunblock, for situations of prolonged exposure, helps to stem the effects of sunburn.

## STORAGE IDEAS

Storage is a major concern aboard all vessels; the smaller the boat, the less storage. The most important way to maximize your storage is to keep your boat clean and well organized. Using individual boxes, sealed against the elements, is helpful to keep items in storage lockers separate from each other. Label all boxes with a permanent marker in clear type.

Hammocks that are strung from the overheads are excellent storage for soft items such as fruit and other perishables.

Consider building wooden racks within storage lockers to keep stored items from being in constant contact with the bottom of the locker. This also keeps air circulating through the items, keeping them from becoming mildewed.

Post a storage map on a bulkhead in your boat, indicating where all items are stored – tools, food storage, emergency repair kit, abandon ship bag. Keep it updated with any changes you make.

## GOING INTO THE WATER

There will be times when you will need to consider going into the water, whether for maintenance, checking the condition of equipment below the waterline, or diving on an anchor to check how well it is set. The most important consideration when considering entering the water is the temperature.

In so-called temperate areas, the frigid waters will give you hypothermia in a matter of minutes. To protect yourself against the cold, consider wearing a wetsuit, which will keep you warm – like a seal in his blubber – even in breathtakingly cold water. In tropical

## Dock line

Dock lines should be made of nylon rope, which stretches, and have an eye splice on one end.

waters, a 'shorty' wetsuit is helpful, even in temperatures of as high as (or even higher than) 25°C (80°F).

If the water is especially cold – as is the case in northern New England, the Pacific Northwest, the Canadian Maritimes, and the British Isles, for example – you might consider buying further protection against the cold: neoprene gloves, 'booties', and even a hood. If you're distracted by the cold while underwater, you will not work as efficiently and you also risk injuring yourself or damaging the boat.

There are several styles of wetsuit available, from the shorty to the Farmer John, which is a two-piece suit – a pair of neoprene overalls and a jacket that usually secures between the legs.

A good mask and snorkel should be considered standard equipment on just about any boat - except for small sailing dinghies. In certain circumstances, you will need to see underwater: if your boat is equipped with an inboard engine, you will probably foul your propeller on fishing line or seaweed at some point. You don't need scuba tanks or an air compressor with over-board hoses to do most quick underwater maintenance tasks, such as clearing a fouled propeller; using a snorkel just takes a bit of practice.

A mask and snorkel are also helpful when checking the anchor to determine how well it is set. To 'dive' on an anchor, follow your anchor rode down or swim on the surface to the spot where your anchor is set. Take a deep breath, and dive straight to the bottom. If the water is not too deep, you may be able to dive down and set your anchor better by hand or clear a foul - such as a rock jammed

# First-aid kit

Each vessel should be equipped with a waterproof first-aid kit. A kit should include, but not be limited to, the following items:

A. First aid handbook
B. Latex gloves
C. Waterproof container
D. Anti-seasickness medication
E. Bandages
F. Medical tape
G. Anti-bacterial soap

H. Anti-bacterial ointment
I. Cotton balls
J. Matches
K. Scissors
L. Epinephrine kit
M. Sterile gauze pads
N. Surgical clamps
O. Tweezers
P. Thermometer
Q. Pen light

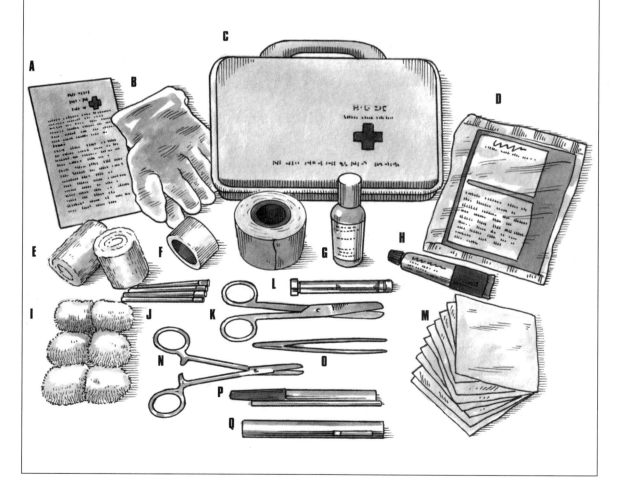

# Storage tips

Consider how your vessel can be improved with better storage ideas. A hammock (A) is useful for hanging from a cabin's overhead; winch handles should be stowed securely (B), so as not to be allowed to fall overboard when a boat heels; and books can be stored on shelves with removable holding racks (C).

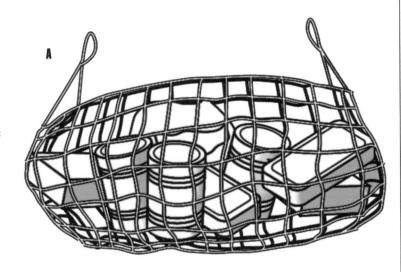

A

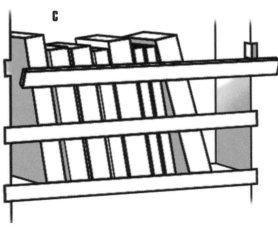

B

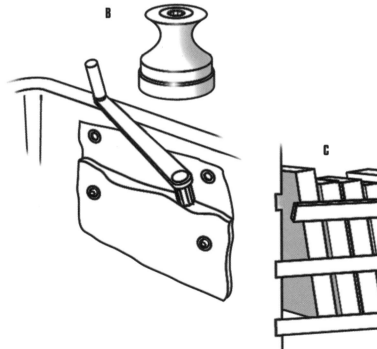

C

in a fluke or a tangle of chain around the anchor. Always use extreme caution when diving on an anchor: the very last thing you want is to become entangled in an anchor's chain or flukes when you are 6m (20ft) below the surface.

A mask and snorkel are also convenient for scrubbing the algae off the bottom of the boat. In areas of heavy marine growth, you will find that your boat accumulates a green 'beard' or tags of mussels. Go over the side wearing a mask and snorkel, and carrying a scrub brush. To combat heavy growth, you may need a putty knife – just be careful not to scratch the hull. To clear a fouled propeller, a fixed-blade knife is especially useful. If you do not have a sailing or filleting knife, a serrated bread knife will suffice. Be extremely careful with any open blades underwater. If you are wearing gloves, your sense of touch will be significantly impaired, increasing the likelihood of self-inflicted wounds.

When stepping off a boat in a mask and snorkel, adjust the mask and snorkel to fit before you get into the water. Then hold your mask tightly to your face and step – don't dive – into the water. You will undoubtedly take some water into your snorkel when you enter the water; simply blow hard, expelling the water, before breathing in air at the surface.

Flippers – or 'fins' – make diving and swimming much easier. By making powerful kicks, you can propel yourself far deeper than if you are simply barefoot. Make sure that fins fit your feet snugly, adjusting any straps before you go into the water.

A word of caution: whenever you go over the side, be sure to have another crew member on deck be your 'buddy'. That person will watch for your safety and can also serve as a 'go-fer' – to retrieve more tools or be an extra set of hands.

It may be helpful to rig one or two lines around the boat, passing over the cabin top and then under the keel, so that the person in the water can follow the line down to the keel or propeller area. This line should be extremely tight.

# CHAPTER 4

# Communication

There are many aspects of sailing, all of which require communication. First, there is communication between a crew. Every member of the crew should be aware of the boat's intended progress, its current condition, the trim of the sails, the weather it is experiencing, and its position in relation to land and other vessels. This is the most basic level of communication, and it is important that the skipper and crew work to ensure that everyone is kept informed.

The other form of communication is boat-to-boat. This is accomplished in a variety of ways, described below. An ability to communicate effectively involves combining certain skills with specific pieces of equipment: if you do not know how to operate a VHF radio or an Internet-capable laptop computer, it is useless.

E-mail communication is also possible, but the scope of this book is primarily focused on near-coastal sailing, where e-mail communication is not as ubiquitous – or necessary – as when sailing offshore. This chapter is primarily concerned with the communication gear necessary to the safe operation of a small sailboat. Each country has different public resources and varied laws regarding communication devices and protocol. It is impossible to provide information on all of these scenarios; the responsibility for determining local laws – and customs – is left to the reader.

As mentioned many times throughout this book, one of the best ways to learn is to ask others in the area about local custom. For example, people who have local experience can offer advice on which 'working channels' are used on the VHF by which marinas; which channels are used by certain commercial fleets; and whether it is customary to use call signs in a given area.

## INTER-CREW COMMUNICATION

At the risk of stating the obvious, it is imperative for the safety of boat and crew alike that a crew is communicating effectively.

Gone are the days of the stoic captain sharing nothing with his helpless crew who, under penalty of death, may not question the decisions of the skipper. Crew members who feel uninformed – out of the loop, so to speak – will feel alienated, but, more importantly, will be less likely to be able to help in the operation of the boat. Ignorance, whether the result of crew members feeling uncomfortable on the boat, lacking the skills to understand the whole picture, or not being properly informed by the skipper,

### High-tech gear

Logging on to the Internet, either at home or via a wireless or satellite connection, offers immeasurable access to weather information and local features for navigation. If you don't have Internet access on your boat, you can download certain programs at home, then take the computer to the boat.

means that they become a liability – to both themselves and others.

It is the skipper's responsibility to familiarize new crew with the operation of the boat and the location of all safety gear, including life jackets, fire extinguishers, communication equipment, and man-overboard (MOB) equipment. Point out certain hazardous areas of the boat: the steepness of a companionway ladder or a low boom, for example. Remember, too, that if the vessel is equipped with a head (marine toilet), each crew member should understand both how it works, whether by a foot pedal flush or a hand lever, and the importance of not putting foreign objects into the toilet, such as paper towels. This will avoid the unpleasant and time-consuming task of fixing a clogged sewage hose.

At the start of the voyage, whether an hour's sail or a three-day cruise, the skipper should inform each crew member of his intentions. Such a briefing should include the expected weather and sea conditions, direction of the wind, and potential route. Recognizing that a sailboat's actual route is often unknown at the start of the voyage, it is still helpful to offer a general description of the surrounding geography and possible routes. If you are a crew member on a friend's boat, be sure to ask for this information before heading out. It will give you peace of mind, allowing you to have a more enjoyable experience. And, in the event of an emergency, you'll be glad you did.

Communication is especially important during times of high excitement, such as anchoring, picking up a mooring, docking alongside, or reefing or striking sails. Crew members should understand, in advance, that there will be many different forces at work: the flapping of the sails, the jerky motion of the boat, and the close proximity of unforgiving objects such as docks or other vessels. As much as possible, the skipper should explain her thoughts on how to carry out these manoeuvres, allowing time for questions. Each crew member should understand how each piece of equipment works and what its significance to the whole manoeuvre represents. Rushing into an anchorage or berth with an uninformed crew that is expected to understand how to handle the anchor tackle or throw a dock line is asking for trouble.

Marina employees are fond of recounting endless stories of vessels that approach a dock with an unprepared crew, the helmsman screaming, crew fumbling with coils of line that are still wrapped in gaskets, fenders lying uselessly on deck instead of deployed over the side, and a strong wind setting them onto the dock – crunch! A little advance planning goes a long way.

If you are the skipper, make sure that your briefing also explains what the potential dangers are, such as getting fingers or limbs pinched between the boat and the dock, falling overboard from a slippery deck because of a flapping sail, or dropping the anchor too soon. If you are the crew member, ask what the specific dangers are, both to yourself and to the boat.

Hand signals between crew, especially between a helmsman and a person on the foredeck handling sail or anchor gear, are especially helpful during rough weather or difficult manoeuvres. Work them out in advance – do not expect that your foredeck crew member will intuit that your thumb-down signal means that you want her to drop the anchor; she might think that you want her to put it away.

## VHF RADIO

The most common type of radio for ship-to-ship communication is the VHF radio. It is not necessary to understand the various bands of radio waves to effectively use a VHF, but this brief description of the radio spectrum will help you to understand what the limits are.

Very high frequency (VHF) radio waves are defined as being between 30 and 300 kHz. What this means for the average user is that this band is useful for clear communication at a limited range, usually line-of-sight. This does not mean that your radio won't work if it is foggy and you cannot see 30m (100ft) in front of you; just that your antenna and the one connected to the station you're trying to call must be within the same plane of the horizon. Generally speaking, the higher the antenna, the greater the range.

A VHF radio is considered standard equipment for all vessels. It can be used to listen to weather reports – via a specific set of frequencies that can be selected on each radio – and to communicate with other vessels. How do you know which VHF is right for your boat? If your vessel has a rechargeable power source, consider installing a base unit, one that can be mounted on a bulkhead, out of the weather, and hard-wired into the boat. (Be sure to install the correct size of fuse between the radio and battery.)

Mount the antenna high in the rig, being sure that the wire and other attachments points will not chafe against sails or running rigging. A base unit will provide far better range than a handheld radio. While radios draw very little power, be sure to shut down your VHF at the end of the day so that it will not continue to draw power at night.

A handheld VHF radio is an excellent choice for sailors who do not have a power source on the boat. The advantage to a handheld, either as a primary radio or as a secondary radio, is portability. The disadvantage is limited range; plus they can be dropped overboard accidentally. Most handheld radios are not waterproof, although a few are advertised as such. Even if you have purchased a 'waterproof' radio, avoid dunking the device; it is a sensitive electronic system that is as susceptible to rust and corrosion as everything else on a boat. Waterproof

## Using a VHF radio

A VHF radio is an invaluable tool on a boat. VHF Channel 16 is the international distress and hailing channel.

Only use it for the briefest of communication, then switch to a 'working' channel.

bags, which are often custom fit, offer an extra measure of protection against the elements.

### Licensing

Most countries require that you purchase a 'station licence' for your VHF radio. Some countries even require an operator licence for VHF radios. These are formalities that enable governing agencies to maintain a measure of control – and awareness – over the already crowded airwaves. When purchasing a radio for your boat, inquire at the chandlery or consult the literature provided in the radio about local laws.

## VHF RADIO PROTOCOL

Now that you have a radio, it is important to know how to use it. First, don't be intimidated by the quaint-sounding lingo associated with radio communication. Speak slowly and clearly, using simple words in plain English, to communicate your intentions. When preparing to use the radio, be certain that the frequency you are using is clear – free from other conversation – before pressing the transmit button.

Remember, you cannot speak in the typical back-and-forth manner typical of telephone conversation; you need to take turns, waiting until you hear the other person finish their sentence with 'over' or until you hear the signature blip of static that indicates he has released the transmit button.

The following are some guidelines about radio customs, from casual 'hailing' to emergency communication, and these should be heeded whenever possible.

- Do not hesitate to reach for the transmitter to contact other vessels, particularly if you are in doubt about their intentions and therefore in danger of a close-quarters situation or collision.
- If you want to place a call – to contact another vessel about their intentions, for example – be sure the radio is set to Channel 16. Be sure the volume control is turned up high enough that you will be able to hear a response. (You can check the volume easily by briefly turning the 'squelch' control down until you hear static.) When you're certain the frequency is clear, press the transmit button. Speaking slowly and clearly, say the name of the vessel you are trying to reach three times, followed by your own vessel's name. If you do not know the name of the other vessel, describe its characteristics, its location, and its course, identifying your boat in relation to his. For example: 'To the grey-hulled container ship approaching Angel Island on a west-bound course, this is the white-hulled sailboat just off your starboard bow.'
- Do not use Channel 16 for idle chat. Once you have made contact with the other vessel, it is your responsibility, as the person who initiated the call, to suggest a working channel. Just about any channel other than 09, 13, 16, and 22 will suffice.

After finishing your exchange with the other vessel, sign off by saying that you will be switching back to Channel 16: 'Sailing vessel *Odyssey* clear 68, standing by 16.'

### Channel 16

Channel 16 is the internationally recognized distress and hailing channel. All radios should be tuned to Channel 16, as it is through that frequency that safety announcements are made by governing agencies, and it is also the channel used by other vessels to make contact.

To repeat, Channel 16 should not be used for idle chat. Once you have made contact with another vessel, switch to a 'working channel', and continue your conversation there. Even brief conversations on Channel

## Asking for help

Do not hesitate to ask for help, either by making a call via VHF radio or by communicating with another vessel however you can, by shouting or by hand signals, for example.

16 are inappropriate and will often provoke admonishments by coastguard agencies, who closely monitor, and record, all radio exchanges on Channel 16.

## Channel 13

Channel 13 is the bridge-to-bridge channel, the frequency used by ship's bridge crew to communicate with other vessels about their manoeuvres. While recreational vessels should try using Channel 16 to contact a ship, Channel 13 is also available.

As always, listen before you begin transmitting. If you have been monitoring Channel 16 and switch to Channel 13 to make a call, be sure that there is no conversation on that channel before making your call.

## Channel 09

In many parts of the United States, VHF Channel 09 is used as the hailing channel for recreational vessels. The coastguard has officially given up trying to enforce this, but some areas still use this system.

It is therefore advisable for recreational vessels to monitor both Channels 09 and 16, which are the main stations for distress and emergency calls.

## Hoax Calls

Each year, rescue agencies risk their lives responding to what turn out to be hoax calls made over VHF radio. Broadcasting your voice for the maritime world to hear should be always conducted in a respectful and professional manner.

## Passing safely

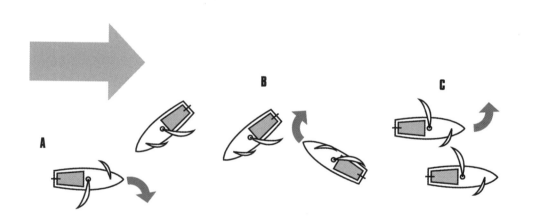

Knowing the Rules of the Nautical Road as they affect the safe navigation of your boat is imperative.

In figure A, the boat on the port gybe should give way to the one on a starboard tack.

In figure B, the same rule applies.

In figure C, both vessels are on a starboard tack, but the vessel on top is overtaking the other and should give way.

If the vessels are proceeding at the same rate, the other vessel should give way because it is the windward vessel.

Under no circumstances should the airwaves be used for practical jokes, however well intentioned. It is not appropriate to let children play with a VHF radio.

## DIGITAL SELECTIVE CALLING (DSC)

Digital selective calling, a feature on new VHF base-unit radios, allows users to place direct calls to another station. The process works like a telephone: you punch in a person's number and their radio 'rings', letting them know that they have a call.

To place a call, type in the person's MMSI number, find a free working channel, then press the 'call' button. Once the party you are trying to reach responds, her radio uses the working channel you have selected. Note that your initial call to the other radio is performed over Channel 70, so most modern radios do not let the user select Channel 70.

The two parties can then carry out a normal VHF radio call, without first having to broadcast a general call to the entire maritime community within range.

While other people can still listen to the exchange if they stumble on your call, this adds an element of privacy to the process and also frees the airwaves, particularly Channel 16, from incessant hailing broadcasts.

In the early days of DSC, sailors worried that they would not be able to make 'all stations' calls – for a Mayday call or in an effort to contact a vessel whose name and number is not known, but which is on a potential collision course. Each DSC radio is

## Mayday calls

When you reach for the radio transmitter to place a Mayday call, you will be anxious. Remember, though, that to receive help, it is important that you convey the necessary information in a clear voice, including as many details as possible.

Deliver the following information all at once, without letting go of the transmit button on the mike:

1. Mayday, Mayday, Mayday.
2. This is [boat name, repeated three times and followed by the boat's call sign].
3. We are located [position in latitude and longitude, or in relation to prominent points of land].

4. We are experiencing [nature of the emergency].
5. Describe the type of assistance that you think you need.
6. Describe the number of people on board, specifying how many are adults and how many children, and whether anyone is injured.
7. Describe your vessel – for example, 6-m fibreglass sailboat with white hull.
8. Repeat the boat name and the channel you will monitor – 16 – then sign off with 'Over'.

Once you have made the call, you will probably be contacted within a few seconds. If not, repeat the process after waiting for a period of two minutes.

If you overhear a Mayday call, do not transmit. First, listen attentively to the broadcast, writing down the information if it will help you remember it. Determine if you are within the area of the vessel in distress. Only if you have determined that your vessel is in a position to offer assistance should you transmit, contacting that vessel in the usual way. Proceed to their location if you believe you are equipped to deal with an emergency.

While you are obliged to render any assistance possible, your obligation ends when your own crew or vessel is in danger.

therefore equipped with an 'all stations' feature, allowing users to use the DSC system and still make general broadcasts.

The United Kingdom Coastguard can receive 'all stations' calls, but the US Coast Guard is not yet 'wired' to do so. To contact the US Coast Guard, use VHF Channel 16 or HF 2182 kHz. However, the DSC system is quickly becoming an international standard, and new equipment reflects this trend.

## RADIO ANNOUNCEMENTS AND EMERGENCIES

A standard set of phrases has been established for effectively making certain types of announcements, whether they describe warnings or emergencies. These are:

**A last resort...**

**Sending messages in a bottle is a fun activity for children and – who knows? – may be used for effective, however slow, communication.**

- 'Mayday', to describe a vessel in imminent distress. It is used to indicate an absolute emergency – such as a sinking, grounding, or other immediate threat to life or property. When making a Mayday call, it is essential to speak slowly and clearly, announcing the name of your boat, describing your position (either in latitude and longitude, or in relation to prominent points of land) and the nature of your emergency.
- 'Pan-Pan' (pronounced 'Pahn-Pahn'), an urgent message that is one step beneath Mayday. A Pan-Pan call is a more urgent general announcement, describing a specific emergency that is not immediately life-threatening. A Pan-Pan call might be

a request for a tow.
- Securité announcements (pronounced Seh-cure-a-TAY), which provide information relating to the weather or navigation. It is the lowest level of warning. Also known as the 'security call' in the United States, this type of verbal VHF message is used to alert other vessels of certain conditions that affect the motion of traffic on a waterway. When spoken by the pilot of a ship, a security call is a general announcement to other vessels navigating in the area. It is intended to alert them to the presence and motion of this vessel.

For example: 'Securité, securité [or

Security call, security call], the laden tanker *Crude Progress* is inbound New York harbour via Ambrose Channel, bound for the Stapleton Anchorage. Concerned traffic please respond on Channel 16 or 13. Tanker *Crude Progress*.' This announcement lets other vessels in the area know what kind of vessel is making the call, where it is located, and where it is bound. The name of the ship is also mentioned one last time before signing off.

## SINGLE SIDEBAND RADIOS

Single sideband (SSB) radios transmit on a slightly lower frequency than VHF, in the HF range, which is 3 MHz to 30 kHz. SSB radios have exceedingly long range transmission and receiving power, capable of communication over a distance greater than 1600km (1000 miles).

For this reason, SSBs are the choice of long-distance sailors, who can use their radios to gather weather information on these bands when they are in the middle of an ocean. Offshore sailors can also communicate with other vessels, who may not be within VHF range, but still within SSB range.

SSB radios are expensive and require professional installation and are not considered standard equipment on small sailboats used on coastal voyages.

## SSB radio

A single sideband radio (SSB) is an effective communication tool for offshore sailors, who need extended range for voice communication and weather broadcasts.

## CELL PHONES

Cell phones are an excellent means of communication for ship-to-shore exchanges for coastal sailboats. Cell phones, like VHF radios, require an antenna within a moderate range. A cell phone uses shore-based towers to relay voice transmissions, which means that, if you're out of sight of land, your cell phone probably won't work. If you're in an area where you have good cell coverage on shore, you will probably find that the same is true when sailing in the adjacent waters, although cliffs and tight coves might serve to block signals.

Cell phones are not usually designed to survive the marine environment. Take extra precautions to keep cell phones away from moisture. Simply put, they will not work if they get

## Inshore communication

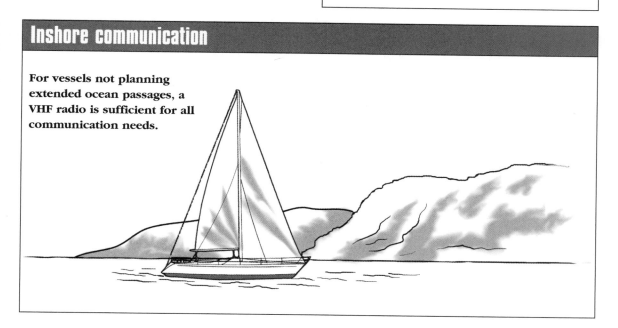

**For vessels not planning extended ocean passages, a VHF radio is sufficient for all communication needs.**

wet. If your vessel is equipped with an electrical system, either 12-volt or 24-volt, consider purchasing a charging adaptor for your cell phone. For just a few dollars, you can purchase a cigarette-style female outlet. These are usually equipped with moisture-resistance covers. You can plug in your cell phone charger adapter – even a laptop. If you do this, however, monitor the charge level of your house batteries. You don't want to leave an object to charge only to find out that you have depleted your boat's batteries.

# CHAPTER 5

# Line and knots

**All rope aboard a vessel is called 'line'. Consider 'rope' as raw material: it comes in large spools from the factory, is still considered rope when it is in the chandlery, and becomes a 'line' only when you have selected it for a desired purpose and cut it to fit. Once it's slung over your shoulder and you're walking out of the chandlery, the rope that was once on the spool is suddenly a line – whether the main sheet, a dock line, or a halyard.**

The learning of knots (and bends and hitches) is an activity to be taken seriously, but do not let yourself become frustrated. Basic knots that are useful aboard boats are simple and easy to learn. The novice sailor will often be intimidated by the fact of (not) knowing his knots and, as a result, create a large tangle in a line in place of a simple knot, unwittingly adhering to the principle, 'If you don't know a knot, tie a lot.' But a tangle has the potential to damage the boat and endanger the crew – far simpler, then, to learn the few turns and tucks that a handful of simple knots require. This chapter will teach you how to tie these few knots, and knowing them will allow you to manage most basic tasks of seamanship that running a small sailboat will require. In general, unless attempting decoration, use the simplest knot; it is probably the best for the task.

If you're interested in learning more about knots, including how to tie decorative and fancy knots, there are numerous volumes available. The most comprehensive is *The Ashley Book of Knots*, published in 1944 and still in print around the world. It is a celebration – a massive, fully illustrated tome – of every conceivable knot in existence.

## Lines

Select the proper line for the job at hand. Three-strand nylon (A) is good for dock lines.

Braided Dacron (B) is an excellent choice for a halyard, as it will not stretch much.

A

B

### THREE-STRAND AND BRAIDED ROPE

Twisted, or laid, rope has been made for thousands of years. Twisted rope is typically composed of three strands that are twisted tightly, usually clockwise, so that the twist holds the rope together. Traditionally made of manila and cotton, the raw material of twisted rope today is mostly man-made.

Braided rope, which has a core and an outer, braided fibre skin, is common for recreational use. It is easier on the hands than twisted rope because of its soft – and more even – outer layer. For better or worse, twisted rope tends to stretch more than braided rope.

Both braided and twisted rope are made of many different materials, including Dacron, nylon, and polypropylene. There are also many high-tech fibres that are available for the performance-oriented sailor, such as Kevlar and Spectra. These are extremely lightweight and do not stretch, making them more akin to steel wire in this way, except that they are supple like other rope fibres.

The following is a description of the basic rope types in use today. The man-made ropes listed are designed both to be strong and to resist rot from moisture and ultraviolet (UV) decay.

### 1. Polypropylene

Polypropylene, also called 'polypro' or 'poly', is an all-purpose, inexpensive rope that has a distinctive, plastic-like feel. It stretches, making it unsuitable for use as running rigging. It can be used for docking lines or mooring pennants, but its tendency to become stiff and bristly makes it an unpleasant rope to work with. Polypro does not hold knots well and becomes tangled easily.

One benefit of polypropylene is that it floats. It makes an ideal tow rope, or a passable dinghy painter, for this reason. Another smart use of polypropylene is as a 'heaving line'.

### 2. Nylon

Nylon stretches and does not float. It is more expensive than polypro, but it holds up better against the sun and salt, and maintains a supple feel. Nylon has a slick, slippery look to it when new and is easy to splice, although its slipperiness does mean that a tight splice is a something of a challenge. Nylon is an excellent choice for docking lines, as the stretching will help absorb shock. For this reason, nylon, especially twisted, is also a good choice for anchor rode or mooring pennants.

Twisted nylon can stretch up to 30 per cent of its length (at roughly half of its breaking strength) and still be undamaged. Braided nylon stretches less, approximately 15 per cent.

### 3. Dacron (Terylene)

Dacron does not stretch very much, making it an excellent candidate for running rigging

## Tying alongside

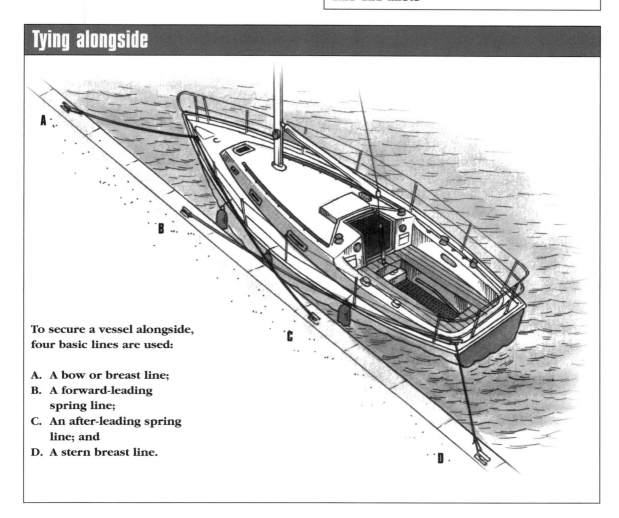

To secure a vessel alongside, four basic lines are used:

A. A bow or breast line;
B. A forward-leading spring line;
C. An after-leading spring line; and
D. A stern breast line.

such as sheets and halyards. It stays supple to the touch and has good UV-resistant qualities. Dacron, whether twisted or braided, stretches about 10 per cent of its length at half its working load. Dacron is also easy to splice. Because it is not slippery like nylon, Dacron splices will hold together well.

### 4. Manila

While not as common as even 20 years ago, manila line can still be purchased at many chandleries. A natural fibre, manila is not as strong as today's modern synthetics, but its distinctive feel and exceptional handling characteristics make it a pleasure to work with and enhance the ambience of any classic boat. Manila is easy to splice, but it swells when wet, making knots difficult to remove and making the line jam in sheaves. Manila should be inspected frequently for rot and wear.

### DOCK LINES

Any boat (excepting small dinghies such as Lasers, 420s, and Sunfish) should have at least four lines dedicated to securing the vessel to a dock. Nylon rope is an excellent choice for making dock lines, as the inherent stretch in the line, especially if it is twisted rope, will make the arrangement less jerky. (Note that Dacron line will not stretch.)

Each dock line should have an eye splice in one end and a whipping in the other. When approaching a dock, always cast the eye of the line to the person on the dock, and direct her to pass the eye around a cleat

## Heaving lines and monkey fists

A 'heaving line' is a lightweight line that is weighted on one end with a 'monkey fist' and, on the other end, secured to a dock line. Heaving lines are handy to use when you are approaching a dock in windy conditions or in tight quarters. By securing a heaving line to your dock line – which is heavier and much more difficult to throw for any great distance – you can incorporate the assistance of people on the dock to assist in your docking manoeuvres.

To set up a heaving line, first tie off your monkey fist to one end of a 15-m (50-ft) length of line. Polypropylene is a sensible choice for use as a heaving line because it floats. Anyone who has docked a boat in difficult circumstances can appreciate the number of times that the dock line seems to land just short of the dock and promptly sink out of reach of the person on the dock. A heaving line should be lightweight line, no more than about 6–10mm (1/4–3/8in) thick.

Tie the other end of the heaving line to the eye splice of your dock line using a slippery rolling hitch. Before the actual approach, the person handling the line should set up the docking line so that it will not foul as it runs out to the dock. Once the heaving line and dock lines are set up, make a neat coil in the heaving line, then split the coil so that half of it is in one hand and the other half – the one with the monkey fist – is in your throwing hand.

The command from the skipper or helmsman should be something along the lines of 'Toss it when you can' – that is, when you think you are close enough to the dock to

actually reach it with a toss. When you toss, imagine that you're throwing a discus. This is a side-arm throw, one that requires plenty of room to swing. Throw the line in a high arc in the general vicinity of the person on the dock. Don't try to hit her with the line; try to throw the line past her so that she can catch the line as the monkey fist sails on past. (You don't want to nail her with the monkey fist; then she's no good to you whatsoever, lying unconscious on the dock.)

Instruct the dock person to do no more than place the eye splice of the dock line around the dock cleat or bitt. Many dock hands, in attempts to be helpful, will attempt to haul your boat when they have captured a line. It is far easier for the boat crew to manage the difficult procedure of bringing the boat alongside with the use of lines. Besides, they are more likely to hear the commands of the helmsman than a person on the dock.

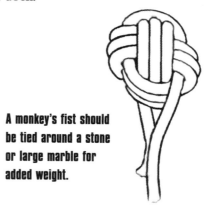

A monkey's fist should be tied around a stone or large marble for added weight.

or post. Placing the splice around the post enables the crew of the boat to apply tension or ease the line in a manner that is consistent with what the helmsman or skipper requires.

Always set up your dock lines in advance of the actual manoeuvres, picturing how the lines will ultimately be configured when the boat is resting alongside the dock. Consider using chafe gear at the hawse holes or chocks if a harbour is especially active and wave action extreme.

## CHAFE

If allowed to rest and rub against another object, line will begin to chafe. If allowed to chafe long enough, the individual fibres of the rope become lacerated, and the rope will eventually cut through. Guarding against chafe is a constant worry aboard a boat. You should prevent or guard against chafe whenever possible.

Dock and mooring lines are especially prone to chafe. When a vessel is alongside, it will roll and pitch, causing the lines to be drawn up tight, and then slack, and then tight again. This back-and-forth motion causes the lines to chafe against the hawseholes. Even a relatively secure dock space can cause chafe in dock lines if the lines are not rotated or protected.

## Rafting alongside

When rafting up with another vessel, you can utilize the other vessel's anchor, provided weather conditions are benign – just be sure that fenders are placed appropriately.

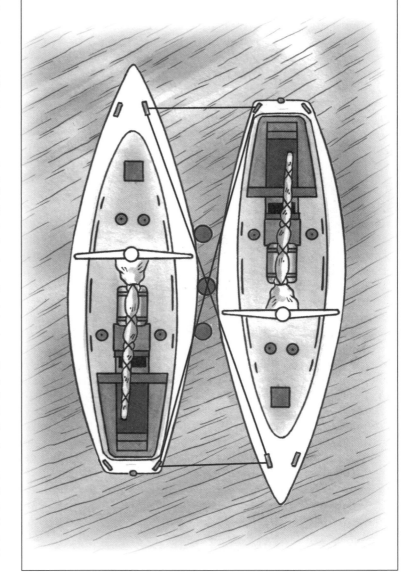

How to guard against chafe? There are several methods, depending on the function. Most involve introducing a sacrificial layer of fabric. Canvas or surplus fire hose – which is canvas on the outside and rubber on the inside – can be wrapped around the line in the area where it will chafe against the boat, thereby protecting the rope itself. Fire hose is an excellent option; the rubberized interior grips well against the rope, but the fabric exterior slides on the hawse. Expired hose can often be procured from fire stations; a hose that may be retired from fighting fires for safety reasons, still makes excellent chafe protection.

Chafe can also take place in the boat's rig. Sails can chafe against running backstays or other running rigging; sheets can chafe against lifelines. Even sheaves chafe the lines

## A note on terminology

- To 'make off' a line is to tie it off to a cleat, a pin, or a post.
- To make it 'fast' is to finish the job, securing the hitches in such a way that the line will not slip.
- To 'reeve' a line is to pass it through another object – a grommet or sheave, for example.
- One should always make off a line with a 'fair lead'. A fair lead is when you bring a line to a cleat or pin in the fairest (simplest) manner. The first turn of the line will be most secure. There is usually one clear way to wrap a line around a cleat or pin, and that is the fair lead.

A fair lead is one way to combat the sailor's nemesis: chafe. If a line crosses over itself in a way that will allow chafe, consider leading it another way. If a line chafes against another, consider using a snatch block to make a fair lead.

they serve just by being in constant contact at the same part of the line. It is often advisable to 'end-for-end' a boat's running rigging – this means reversing the line so that different sections of the same line come to bear on the sheaves. Halyards and sheets are both good candidates for an end-for-end treatment. Just be sure to use a secure tag line when doing this with a halyard; otherwise, it will be necessary to send a person aloft to re-route the line.

## A round turn

A round turn is an extra turn in a line, taken around a ring or grommet, which distributes the load on the line where it is in contact with the ring. A round turn is used as chafe protection.

## Baggywrinkle

Although it sounds like a disparaging term for a person who is getting on in years, baggywrinkle actually refers to traditional chafe gear that is installed in a boat's rig. When sails come to bear against running backstays or shrouds, they chafe, potentially wearing holes or creating weak spots in the fabric. Clumps of fuzzy baggywrinkle secured to a boat's standing rigging eliminate – or at least significantly reduce – the amount of chafe that occurs as a result of this strain.

To make a baggywrinkle, secure both ends of a 2.5-m (8-ft) length of 6-mm (3/8-in) line to a stationary object. (If you're doing this on your boat, secure the line to the lifelines or between the shrouds.) Cut up a three-strand rope in numerous 20-mm (8-in) sections. Unlay the rope sections so that you are left with a large pile of the individual strands. Now, using a cow hitch, secure these strands, one at a time, to the longer line that you have secured between your shrouds, beginning at one end and working down the line. Each successive cow hitch should be tied snugly against the one previously laid on.

Once you've created a 2–2.5-m (6–8-ft) section of this hairy mass, it is time to install it in the rig. Using a bosun's chair, hoist yourself into the rig, and seize one end of this line to the shroud in the area where chafe is likely to occur. Now wrap the baggywrinkle around the shroud tightly, completely covering the shroud so that the strands all stick straight out from the shroud. Once you've finished, seize the bottom of the baggywrinkle securely to the shroud as you did the upper end.

## TO LOCK OR NOT TO LOCK

Each time you make a line off to a cleat or pin, you will wrap several figures of eight. On a belay pin, three turns is considered standard; any more and you will be making a mess.

Should you use a locking hitch? A locking hitch is made by flipping the bight (loop) of a line over on itself when making it off to a cleat or a pin. It is a very secure arrangement, and, if made tight enough, it will not slip. But is one needed every time? This depends on the boat and on how secure a line is without a locking hitch, but the standard on working sailing ships involves using a locking hitch only when there is a man aloft, whose life depends on the line being secure.

## Locking hitch

A locking hitch, a hitch that buries the working end of the line on the last turn, is appropriate for use on docking lines and on a 'gantline', a line used to raise a person aloft. A locking hitch should not be used on halyards and sheets, which need to be secured in such a way as to allow hurried removal.

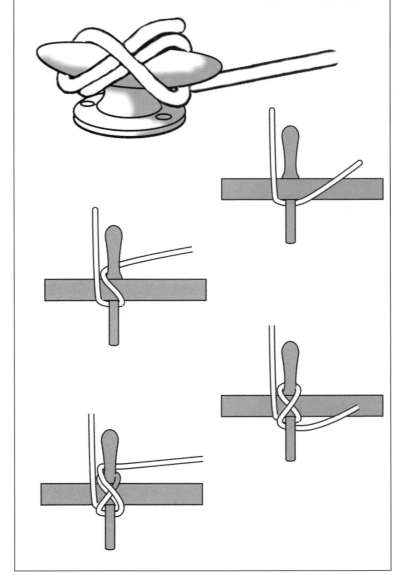

85

Many vessel skippers choose not to use locking hitches on sheets and halyards, the theory being that, if the line is to be taken off in a hurry (as in a knockdown or approaching squall), a locking hitch will unnecessarily slow the process. But using a locking hitch on a 'gantline' – a line used for raising a person aloft – will give pause to anyone who might be working on deck, tidying lines. If she sees a locking hitch on a line where there is strain, she'll be less likely to simply cast it off. (At least, that's the idea.)

A locking hitch may also appropriate for use on docking lines or on lines which are secured to a cleat that might be too small to make enough wraps to be fully secure.

## THE BITTER END

While it may sound like the name of a rough-and-tumble bar for sailors, the bitter end actually refers to the end of a length of line. Most lines, whether sheets or halyards, have a standing end – the end that is attached to the sail or another object – and a bitter end –

## Some useful tools

Working with rope can involve the use of a few basic hand tools:

- A marlinespike is a pointed piece of tapered steel, which can be used to open the cant of the line for a splice, to tighten a knot, or as a lever for loosening shackles. Most marlinespikes have a flattened tip like a slotted screwdriver, making them easy to slip between knots and strands of rope.
- A fid is a wooden marlinespike. A Swedish fid is a hollowed-out fid with a metal shaft, which makes splicing easier. It can be used to open a gap between two strands of rope, leaving the hollow channel to insert another strand. Swedish fids typically have wooden handles for comfort.
- A knife is an essential tool for seamanship and linehandling. A knife with a fixed or locking blade will work best, as it will not collapse on your fingers. Keep the edge sharp, as a dull blade is more dangerous – and far less useful – than one with a keen blade. A serrated edge will cut through line quickly, but the edge is difficult – nigh impossible – to sharpen without specialized equipment.
- A pair of slim pliers with gripping teeth is

often helpful when working with knots and splices.
- A leather palm, which fits over the user's dominant hand, is like a giant thimble. It is used to press large sailmaker's needles through heavy canvas or rope. The palm's metal cup is grooved to hold the head of the needle.
- A sailmaker's needle is a heavy steel sewing needle for repairing sails and whipping the ends of line or making seizings. The needle's tip is usually shaped in an elongated triangle, the edges being sharp for cutting through the fabric. A sailmaker's needle has a large eye for heavy thread.
- A chuck of natural beeswax can be used to protect twine or thread when repairing sails or whipping lines. Run the thread through the block of wax before sewing. The wax will also hold stitches together, keeping the repairs tight and strong.
- A cigarette lighter is useful for burning the ends of rope so that the fibres melt together and therefore cannot unravel.
- Plastic electrical tape is useful for holding the ends of rope together when performing whippings or splices. Remove the tape when a splice or whip is completed.

an end that is not attached to anything.

## MAKING A COIL

Coils should always be made clockwise. To coil a halyard after a sail is set, grab the line at the standing end with one hand – your left if you are right-handed. Draw out a length of line with the right hand, giving it a half turn in a clockwise direction with your fingers as you make a bight. Grab the new loop with your left hand, and repeat the process. The half turn works the twists out of the line. The loops should all be the same size – large enough that you aren't left with an enormous pile of line and small enough that the loops don't spill all over the deck. Traditionally, lines were coiled in such a way as to not touch the deck when they were hung on a pin.

To hang a coil on a pin or a cleat, reach one hand through the coil, grabbing a bight from the standing end and pulling it through the coil. Turn the bight over once in your hand before capturing the coil and hanging the bight back on a horn of the cleat or on the belay pin.

## A KNOT, A HITCH, OR A BEND?

Most people don't pause to consider the differences between a knot, a hitch, and a bend. While similar in appearance, knots, hitches,

## Knots

Take the time to learn a few basic knots, and use them on your boat. The best knot for the job is the simplest one.

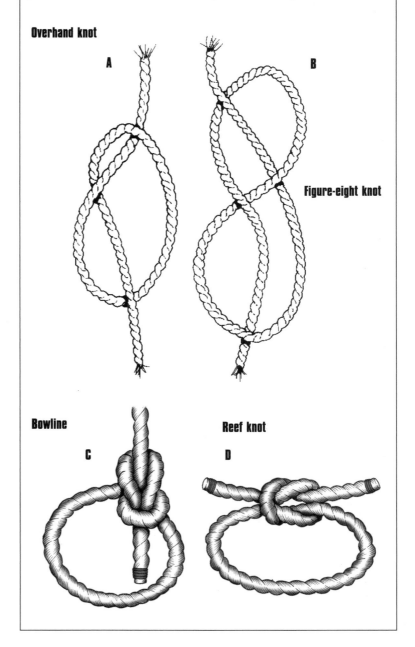

Overhand knot

A

B

Figure-eight knot

Bowline

C

Reef knot

D

and bends differ in function. A bend is a knot that joins two lines together; a hitch is a knot that joins a line to another object such as a post; a knot is anything else.

For example, a bowline is a knot. A rolling hitch, obviously, is a hitch, intended to secure a line round a spar without slipping. And a fisherman's bend is a bend that can be used to secure the ends of two lines together.

## Common knots

### 1. The bowline

This is the most common sailor's knot. Relatively easy to tie – with some practice – the bowline is also easy to untie, even if a heavy load has been imposed on the line. A bowline can be used to secure a sheet to the grommet on the clew of a sail; to secure a downhaul or a halyard; or to make a secure loop in a dinghy painter – indeed, the bowline can be used for just about any purpose where a secure loop is required.

If tying off a bowline for a purpose that might introduce chafe – as on a sheet or a halyard, for example – use a round turn in the bight of the line before securing the bitter end in the tuck.

This will spread out the load of the line and hence reduce any resulting chafe, keeping your line in good condition.

### 2. Reef knot

A reef knot is used to secure the bottom of a

## The stopper knot

Every now and then, you will need to relieve the strain on a line without wanting – or being able – to undo the knot that holds it fast. Imagine, for instance, a sail whose halyard is stuck, a sheet that is hopelessly tangled around a winch and the sail needs to be tacked, but the strain on the sail is too severe to be easily relieved. Enter the stopper knot.

A stopper knot was traditionally used on large sailing ships when a team of sailors were hauling up a heavy sail. There might be eight or ten people all hauling on the line attached to a sail that could weigh 450kg (1000lb) or heavier.

How could a single crew member secure the line when it took as many as 10 people to maintain the strain and keep the sail from dropping back down? Simple: by grabbing a short line, perhaps only 0.9–1.2m (3–4ft) in length, which was spliced to a padeye on the deck.

Using this length of line, he lashed a quick stopper knot to the halyard, then yelled to the gang of haulers to release the line, thereby transferring the strain from their hands to the stopper knot. Next he would make the halyard off on a belay pin, and finally he released the stopper knot.

A line that is expressly meant for this purpose should be modified in the following way: splice an eye in the end of a 1.2-m (4-ft) length of rope, using Dacron, nylon, or whatever else is the standard on the boat. After completing the splice, seize the end of the splice. Now unlay the rest of the line.

Once the line is unlaid all the way back to the seizing, braid – or plait – the three strands back together. A braided or plaited line becomes flattened, a preferable shape for a stopper line. Once fully braided, whip the bitter end of the line in the usual way.

To use the stopper line, simply cow-hitch the splice in place in a way that will take the strain of the line you need to relieve.

sail when it is time to reef. A reef knot – or a 'square knot' in landsman's parlance – is two overhand knots, but the second overhand knot is tied opposite the first. If tied improperly, a 'granny knot' is the result; granny knots are two overhand knots, but they look lopsided.

A reef knot, unlike a granny knot, will always untie easily when the knot is pushed together. A 'slippery' reef knot is when one loop is left in the knot, allowing the knot to remain secure, but also to be pulled out easily.

When securing reefpoints, be sure to secure them between the footrope and the boom, not going around the base of the boom even if the reefpoints are long enough.

### 3. Constrictor knot
Although it is really a hitch, as it is used to secure a line to an object other than a rope – such as a post or a spar – the constrictor knot is a handy knot because it will not slip when tightened, hence the name.

It can be used to temporarily secure a cracked tiller or oar, or simply to tie a line around a pencil so that it won't leave the nav station.

### 4. Figure-of-eight knot
A figure-of-eight knot is tied to the bitter end of a line that you do not want to allow to slip through a block. The figure-of-eight, when drawn up tight, forms a tidy ball at the end of the line, preventing the line from running all way out. This is a helpful knot to tie on the end of a main sheet, for example.

## Common bends

### 1. Sheet bend
The sheet bend is the most widely practised means of joining two lines together. Its simplicity and functionality are perfect.

Begin the knot by passing the working end of one of the lines through the bight of another line. Wrap it around the back side of

## Bends

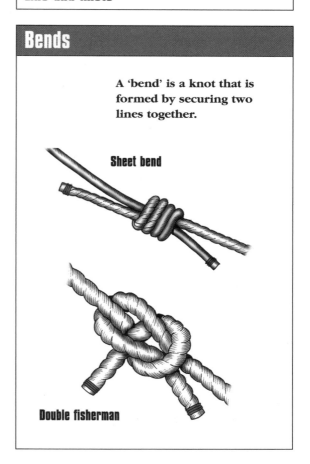

A 'bend' is a knot that is formed by securing two lines together.

**Sheet bend**

**Double fisherman**

the bight, coming back around to the front. Instead of passing the line through the bight again, wrap it under itself, and bring it up to pull tight.

### 2. Fisherman's bend
A fisherman's bend is the simplest bend to make when joining two lines of equal diameter. A fisherman's bend can be made with double or triple wraps.

### 3. Anchor bend
More of a hitch than a bend – a bend is technically a knot that secures two lines to each other – the anchor bend was traditionally used to secure a line to the ring of an anchor. It is fast and easy to set up and will not come undone.

## Common hitches

### 1. Half-hitch

A half-hitch is ubiquitous for its simplicity. It involves making a single turn around the standing end of a line, passing the line back through the bight. Two half-hitches are an excellent choice for securing a fender to a stanchion.

### 2. Clove hitch

A clove hitch is handy to use as an all-purpose hitch for securing a dinghy to a post or pile. The clove hitch will not hold if there is a constant strain – a good alternative would be a pair of half-hitches.

### 3. Rolling hitch

A rolling hitch is a variant of the stopper knot, excellent for securing a line to a post or spar in a hitch that will not slide or release under strain. Be sure that you tie the hitch in such a way that the strain is directed down in the same direction as the hitch's two initial wraps.

### 4. Cow hitch

To make a cow hitch, pass a loop of line around whatever it is you want to secure it to, then pass the bitter end through the loop. The cow hitch can be used to secure a stopper line to a padeye, a tell tale to a shroud, or the numerous strands of line that make up the hairy mass of baggywrinkle.

## SEIZING

To seize a splice is to wrap it with 'small stuff' or twine in such a way as to capture and squeeze the line together. A seizing is

## Rolling hitch

A rolling hitch is a useful way of securing a rope to a pole so that it will not slip.

A. To tie, place the standing part of the rope alongside the pole in the direction opposite to that in which the pole will be moved.

B. Turn the rope twice around the standing part of the pole with the running end.
C. Reverse the standing part of the rope so that it is leading off in the direction in which the pole will be moved.
D. Take two turns with the running end.

E. On the second turn, pass the running end under the first turn to secure it.
F. To make it secure, tie a half-hitch with the standing part of the rope at least 30cm (12in) along the rolling hitch.

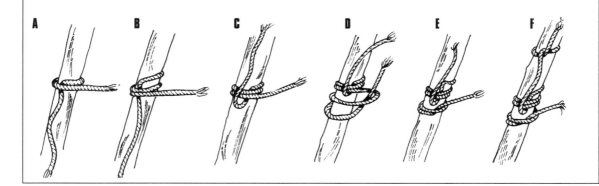

A  B  C  D  E  F

## Hitches

A hitch is a knot that secures a line to an object such as a post or a spar.

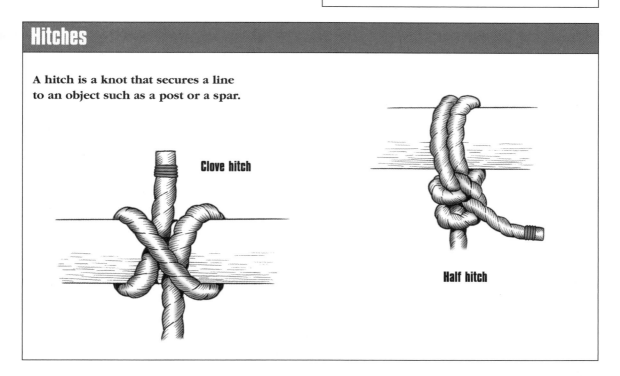

Clove hitch

Half hitch

meant to bring the two parts of a splice together – as when capturing a thimble, for example.

### ROPE CARE

Like every piece of equipment aboard a boat, rope needs to be cared for. This is somewhat less true than in times past, when natural fibre rope could not be stored wet because it would then rot. However, rope is subject to the same laws of physics that affect the rest of the boat, so even the most modern fibre ropes wear out – rope chafes and stretches. It becomes stiff and impossible to splice and difficult to coil.

Inspection of your boat's lines is the best protection against all of these forces. Periodically run each line through your fingers, visually inspecting the entire length, looking for chafed areas or cut fibres. If the rope is twisted rope, twist open the strands and inspect the inside of the rope. If the

strands have become pointed and are worn to the degree that small bits of rope fibre are coming away from the strands, the rope is at the end of its useful life and must be retired.

There is no rule of thumb dictating how often line needs to be replaced, as this is dependent on the environment, the amount of sailing done, and the specific use. But a line should remain supple to the touch and able to be turned comfortably around a pin or cleat, or turned neatly into a coil without feeling stiff.

### WHIPPING

There are two basic methods of making a whip on the end of a line. One involves using a needle to make a secure, long-lasting whip; the other is called the 'quick whip' and can be made without a needle. Both styles of whipping should be made extremely tight so that they cannot become unravelled.

To make a quick whip, make a simple bight in the thread, laying it against and parallel to the line near the bitter end. Now, begin to wrap the thread around the line working from the standing end toward the bitter end so that the whipping of the thread covers the loop of thread that has already been laid down. Make each wrap exceedingly tight, using a marlinespike to tighten the thread if necessary. Continue whipping the line until your whipping measures the same distance as the rope's diameter – for example, make the whip 12mm (1/2in) long if the rope is 12mm (1/2in) in diameter. When you've whipped far enough, pass the end of the thread through the loop, then draw the loop up tight so that the loop is drawn under the whipping. Cut the thread at both ends so that the loop is buried beneath the whipping.

To make a more permanent whipping, begin the whip in the same manner, but remember that a loop is unnecessary. Whip the line to the same distance as the rope's diameter, then use the needle to bring the line back across the whipping, following the cant (groove) of the line. Perform two of these 'frappings' for each of the rope's three cants; then bury the end of the thread and cut it off closely.

After a whipping is completed, it helps to burn the end of the line – if the rope is man-made – so that the fibre ends will melt together.

## SPLICING THREE-STRAND ROPE

If a line is going to be permanently used with a bight of line in the same place, it makes sense to splice the loop. All knots weaken the rope's overall strength. A splice done properly recovers some of that strength. Plus, a splice is smooth and attractive. If a splice is being used in the rigging and a small, concentrated strain is going to be imposed on the loop, consider using a thimble in the splice. A thimble is a rounded metal or nylon ring that is formed to fit the inside of a splice. Be sure that the thimble you select is of the same diameter as the line with which it will be used. Otherwise, the thimble will fall out – probably at the worst possible moment.

Splicing is confusing for the first few times it is attempted. There are a few rules of thumb to learn:

● Three-strand rope is spliced by sending the strands against the lay of the line. You want to splice such that all three strands are advanced together – that is, tuck one strand once, then tuck the others in turn.

## Splicing a three-strand rope

Splicing a three-strand rope is a basic skill with numerous uses aboard a boat of any size. The first step (A) is to select the size of the eye. Next unlay the rope a few inches (B), before beginning to splice the strands back into the standing part of the line (C). Always splice against the lay of the rope (D), and finish off with a taper (E).

A      B      C      D      E

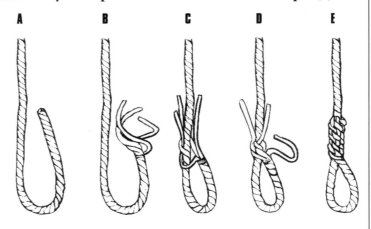

## Making a wash-down bucket pennant

Every boat should be equipped with a bucket for gathering seawater. Choose the traditional wood-bottomed, collapsible canvas bucket, which stores easily, or use a plastic or rubber masonry bucket. Do not use a metal bucket, however, as it will rust and scratch the side of the hull.

To make a pennant for a bucket using three-stand rope, first tie a clove hitch to the handle on one end of a 2.5-m (8-ft) length of line – Dacron, nylon, or manila. (The two loops of the clove hitch will spread out the chafe area.) Now unwrap the working end of the line, and splice it back into the standing end. Tying single overhand knots into the line at regular intervals (say, every 60cm/2ft) will ease the raising of the bucket onto the deck of the boat. Finish the end of the line with an eye splice or a decorative knot.

Be sure to have a firm grip on the bucket's leash when throwing it over the side. If the boat is moving at all, the bucket will act as a giant sea anchor and can pull you over the side or at the very least slip from your grasp. Always use extreme caution when bringing a bucket aboard.

- Don't try to make all the tucks on a single strand first. A basic splice involves tucking each of the strands three times. The outcome of this should be that all three strands emerge from the standing end of the line at the same place in the line.
- To finish the splice, advance one of the tucks one more time beyond where the basic splice was finished, then advance a second strand two more times beyond the end of the splice. This produces a splice with a tapered look. Another method is to continue to tuck all the strands in the same method as the splice, but not before cutting a percentage of the strand with a knife. By the time three more tucks are made with each strand, the splice will have a long, even taper both attractive and functional in its design.

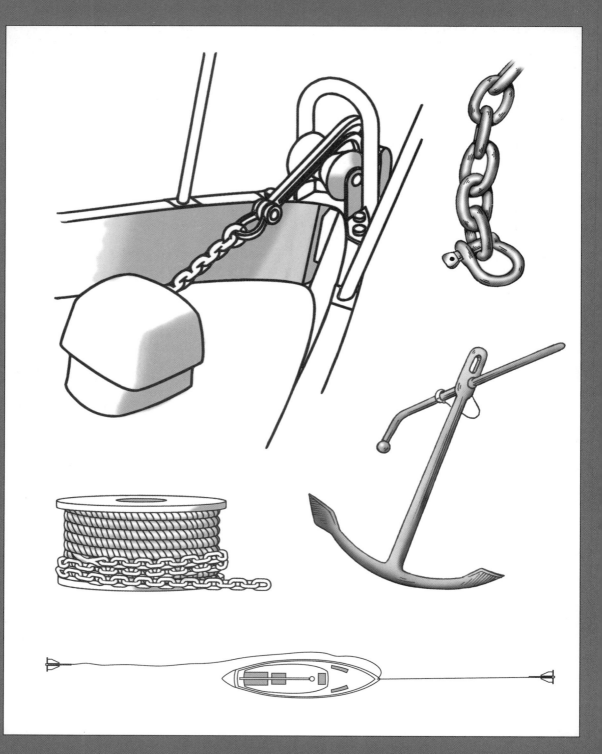

# CHAPTER 6

# Anchoring and mooring

Anchoring a vessel and mooring alongside a dock are manoeuvres that often fill the inexperienced mariner's heart with dread. How quickly will your vessel slow after you have rounded it into the wind? How well will it back down when it is brought to a dock? Will all the lines be ready? Will the fenders be in the correct position to provide good protection between the hull and dock?

Bringing a moving vessel in close proximity to a hard object – whether it be a dock, other anchored vessels, or rocky ledges – involves understanding how a vessel interacts with these objects.

The secret to successful anchoring and mooring is the same as with other manoeuvres aboard a boat: preparation. There are currents and winds to contend with; the crew to confer with; and the mooring equipment to consider. Anchoring or mooring is hard enough for even expert boathandlers under the best circumstances – so be prepared.

## A FEW WORDS ON SAFETY

Before discussing the types of anchors available to the small sailboat operator, safety must first be considered. Anchors are large, heavy objects that will sink straight to the bottom when dropped overboard. If you are handling an anchor on the foredeck, always be sure to keep your feet, legs, and arms free of the anchor rode – the rope or chain that holds an anchor to the boat – as it will shoot over the side with great speed as soon as the anchor is released. Under no circumstances should you wrap the rode around your arm to lower the anchor into the water, for example.

Be aware that the foredeck of a vessel is narrow and can often be wet and slippery. When communicating with the helmsman, the person on the foredeck should be sure to speak loudly and clearly, as the helmsman may not be able to hear well if the engine is running or the sails are flapping. It might be sensible to develop a set of hand motions to facilitate communication between the helmsman and foredeck crew: thumb down for dropping the anchor, a closed fist to make the line fast, a wagging finger to let out more line, and so on. Ensure that the signals are different enough from each other that they cannot be confused.

## THE ANATOMY OF AN ANCHOR

Every anchor has flukes, the sharpened bladelike extensions that serve to sink into the bottom and secure a

## Weighing anchor

Handling an anchor is a tricky affair. An anchor is heavy and cumbersome, and the foredeck is narrow and can be slippery, especially when wet. Foredeck crew should use extreme caution when handling the anchor, even in calm conditions.

vessel in position. Flukes come in many different shapes, but the purpose is the same. Every part of the anchor and ground-tackle that is effectively upstream of the flukes – including the shank, ring, rode, and attachments on the deck of the boat – serve to assist the flukes in holding on to the bottom. The flukes on some anchors can swivel at the crown – as on a Danforth or some ploughlike anchors – and these are attached to the anchor's shank, the vertical section.

Attached to the anchor's shank is the stock, the crossbar that prevents the anchor from lying on its side and also assists the flukes in remaining point-down in the bottom. There are now stockless anchors – made possible by the development of the swivelling fluke and plough anchors that are common today – but traditionally stocks were necessary for holding power. Indeed, they were the technology that held anchors to the bottom. Traditional, or fisherman, anchors are still in use today, but most mariners choose to select an anchor of a more specialized design and lighter weight that works well in the specific environment where most of the sailing is to be done.

When an anchor is well set in the bottom, it may be difficult to retrieve. Some anchors are equipped with rings at the crown (between the flukes), and these can be used to attach a trip-line for ease of retrieval. Attach one end of the line to this ring and the other end to a buoy. After being secured, the buoy is cast into the water to be picked up when the anchor is retrieved. The length of line should be the same as the depth of the water, accounting for the rise of the tide.

## TYPES OF ANCHORS

Before selecting an anchor style for your boat, it is prudent to ask around or take a walk by the local marina, to observe the style of anchors chosen by others in the area. Consult charts of the area, and read the bottom descriptions. Find out if the bottoms are mostly sand, whether seagrass is common, and whether there is mud at the bottom or rocks. Such investigation will yield some valuable information on local anchoring conditions and popular anchorages.

### Fisherman, or traditional, anchor

In the old days, traditional anchors were secured to the rail of a ship or yacht at the bows and lashed in place with the flukes positioned aft and the anchor's ring lashed to a cathead – a protrusion that allowed the anchor to hang away from the hull when about to be deployed. While this is an attractive arrangement, it is not always necessary with traditional anchors used today, many of which have removable stocks for easy, flat stowing on deck. Because of their all-purpose function, heavy traditional anchors serve well as reserve or storm anchors. They also work well in areas of heavy grass or kelp.

### Plough anchor

Developed in the United Kingdom under the brand name CQR – say this quickly, and it sounds like 'secure' – the plough anchor has since gone through several developments. Plough anchors lack a stock and are therefore easy to stow on the bow of a boat, preferably on rollers. Some plough anchors – the CQR and Fortress anchors included – have a pivot near the crown, allowing the flukes to remain set in the bottom and the shank to swivel as the boat moves around in the waves.

A Bruce anchor has an extended crown and three flukes. The height of the crown means that these flukes can roll into position and dig into the bottom from any angle of pull from the rode. Plough anchors are effective in sand and mud bottoms.

### Lightweight anchor

The most common type of lightweight anchor is the Danforth. With its long, flat flukes that swivel in either direction, the lightweight anchor holds well in hard, sandy bottoms. Their light weight means that these anchors require a great deal of 'scope' – for further discussion of this term, see below. Lightweight anchors can also become easily fouled by debris, such as sticks and rocks, so care should be taken to ensure the anchor is properly set before allowing the boat to be left for any time. Lightweight anchors stow easily and can be lashed to a rail or stowed flat in a locker.

### Mushroom anchor

Small mushroom anchors, so-called because of their shape, are used on small vessels for temporary anchoring. The larger mushrooms, which are nearly impossible to handle or stow on a boat, are popular for use as moorings.

### Sea anchors

There may be times when it is considered prudent to deploy a sea anchor, a parachute-like device that enables a boat to be nearly stopped in the water, head to wind and waves. A sea anchor, which is deployed off the bow, is not to be confused with a drogue, which drops off the stern. A sea anchor is not a traditional anchor, made of metal and featuring a set of flukes, a stock, and a ring. It is made of fabric and works as a sort of parachute-like brake. Sea anchors require a great deal of rode to be effective, and they are equipped with a swivel that allows them to rotate without twisting the line. A sea anchor is not considered standard equipment on a daysailer; it is intended to be used on vessels making offshore passages that are at risk of becoming overwhelmed by the seas.

A great deal of debate exists in the offshore sailing community regarding whether a vessel should be equipped with or a drogue or whether a vessel should be made to heave-to – or avoid storms altogether. While everyone agrees that it is advisable to avoid storms at sea, many argue that sooner or later a person who spends a great deal of time at sea will be greeted by an extreme storm scenario, the result being that he would need to have a plan about how to best deal with the situation at hand. Suffice to say that sea anchors have been used in certain circumstances with success.

If you make the decision to equip your vessel with a sea anchor, be sure that you know exactly how to use it. Take it out of its packaging, and take the time to rig it. Deploy it off the bow in benign conditions. And then practice deploying it in moderate conditions. There are whole books dedicated to the use of sea anchors, which make recommendations about sizing the sea anchor for the vessel, length and size of rode, and how to rig a bridle off the bow. Always follow a manufacturer's instructions carefully, and be sure the deck equipment on your boat can handle the extreme loads that will imposed in storm conditions.

### Drogues

Not to be confused with a sea anchor, a drogue is a device that is towed astern of a vessel at sea. Drogues are meant to slow progress through the water, not arrest it altogether.

In severe storm conditions, when a vessel is making too much way and threatening to broach or even trip end over end, it is crucial to reduce the forward speed of the boat. Essentially, this can be done in whatever manner is possible in the prevailing conditions: desperate mariners have tried streaming the warps – deploying great loops of line astern to create friction through the water and slow the vessel; or even tossing out old tyres on the ends of stout hawsers.

Drogues are specialized equipment for the same purpose. Whatever you stream in such an event, consider the enormous loads on the line. Be certain that the points where you secure the lines – whether on cleats, pad-eyes, or chocks – can bear the strain. You must always follow the manufacturer's instructions carefully.

## Anchor choices

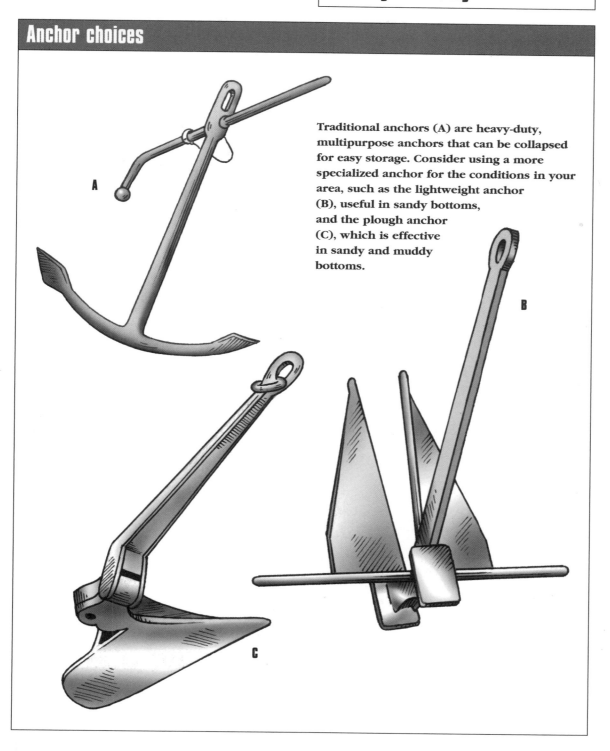

Traditional anchors (A) are heavy-duty, multipurpose anchors that can be collapsed for easy storage. Consider using a more specialized anchor for the conditions in your area, such as the lightweight anchor (B), useful in sandy bottoms, and the plough anchor (C), which is effective in sandy and muddy bottoms.

A

B

C

## Chafe

After being tied to the windlass or a post, the anchor rode will pass through a chock or a hawse pipe before it leads into the water. Whatever comes into contact with the line or chain will cause wear – chafe – on the line. Chafe is a serious problem for an anchored vessel. Indeed, if allowed to wear long enough, a line will chafe through, and the vessel will break free.

To evaluate the level of chafe and guard against it, first be certain that the rode leads fairly over the bow and into the water. If it lies against anything, figure out a way to keep it away, or wrap the line with heavy canvas. Pay particular attention to the bobstay – the wire or chain that leads from the end of the bowsprit, or bow pulpit, down to the base of the bow stem at the waterline. Some vessels are equipped with bow rollers, which keep the line going over the end of the bowsprit and away from all rigging.

A vessel at anchor in a strong current or during heavy winds will be especially subject to chafe; the vessel will want to scoot around on its anchor, sailing back and forth as the wind catches one side, pushing on it until the anchor rode catches and then pushing on the other side. This process will impose dynamic loads on your anchor gear – to solve this, see the box 'Anchoring – a few tricks' on page 107 – and also introduce chafe to the line.

If you find that you need to wrap your line in chafe protection, ensure that you wrap a large enough section of line so that the entire area of rode is protected where it comes to bear against the boat. Use string or heavy-duty tape to secure the canvas to the rode. Check your anchor gear frequently if you are at anchor during rough conditions.

## SIZING AN ANCHOR AND SELECTING GROUNDTACKLE

The appropriate size of an anchor varies with conditions and the specific use it will see. There are some rules of thumb to consider: for example, a lightweight anchor such as a Danforth does not rely on its weight for holding power and is therefore more effective than an anchor of another design of the same weight – provided it is used in the conditions for which it was designed. The weight of an anchor is the first in a series of measurements and calculations that should be done when considering how to outfit a boat with groundtackle.

Most anchors are equipped with a length of chain that is spliced into a soft-line rode. The chain lies on the bottom and is therefore less likely to be damaged by chafe from contact with the bottom than a soft line. Furthermore, the weight of the chain contributes to diminishing the angle, or scope, of the overall rode.

Besides the weight of the anchor itself, one should also consider how much force will be at work on the groundtackle. How high-sided is the vessel? Wind will apply significant force to the hull, often making a vessel sail back and forth on its anchor,

## Anchor rode

An anchor rode often is made up of both chain and nylon line spliced together. The chain adds weight and durability at the anchor end.

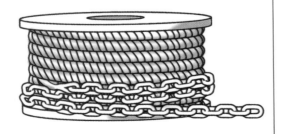

straining the anchor rode and threatening to make the anchor drag.

All components of a vessel's groundtackle – anchor, shackles, the chain, and soft-line rode – and the attachment point on the vessel, such as the bitt or Samson post, should be assembled to exceed the expected working load. (Remember that a system is only as safe as the weakest link.) It is more prudent to select an anchor (and rode) that is slightly larger than expected conditions and the size of the boat might suggest. Similarly, installing more than enough rode will ensure that there is always more line to pay out to increase scope and the anchor's holding power. Having peace of mind about the ability of your ground-tackle to hold your vessel in position, whether stopped for the night or just a quick break ashore for supplies, is not to be underestimated.

## ANCHORAGE

The first element you need to consider when selecting an anchorage is courtesy. The rule of thumb is first come, first served. If there are other vessels in an anchorage area, be sure to keep well clear. While most vessels in an anchorage will swing in the same direction as each other – moved by the wind or current – you still need to ensure that you keep sufficient distance between your anchorage and that of other boats. Keep in mind that, when you drop your

## Chain link

Your ground tackle is only as secure as its weakest link. Always inspect your anchor gear for corrosion and worn components, including the chain's links and the shackle.

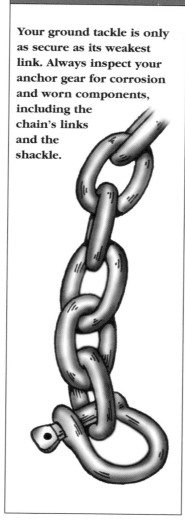

anchor and ease out the rode, your vessel will drift downwind a considerable distance. It is therefore advisable to anchor astern of another vessel already anchored. That way, letting out more line will mean only that you drift further away. If you must drop your anchor upwind (or up-current), you should always carefully consider where you want your boat to rest and then work backwards from there: you'll need to let out enough line to have appropriate scope on the rode, but not so much that you risk bumping into the other vessel.

### Scope

It is not an anchor's weight that holds your vessel in one position over the bottom; it is the design of the anchor and the amount of scope used. When determining an appropriate anchorage, it is imperative that you know the water depth – or, at least, an approximation. From the depth, you will then determine how much 'scope' you will need – that is, the ratio of rode length to the water's depth. The greater the water depth, the more line will be needed. The idea is that the force imposed on the anchor – by the tug of the hull being pushed by wind and waves – must be as near horizontal as practical. If you drop an anchor straight down, it will bounce or drag along the bottom. As you let out more line, it will begin to catch the bottom.

# Good anchorage

A secure anchorage is a wonderful thing, and every sailor's dream. This can involve a combination of factors, including good holding ground such as mud or sand, relatively shallow water, shelter from prevailing wind and swells, and proximity to shore. Your chart will show you where to find good anchorages, as will discussions with other sailors.

The amount of scope necessary is defined by the type of anchor you have and whether you have chain or soft line:

- when using all chain, allow room for a ratio of at least 3:1 (length:depth);
- when using half chain and half nylon, allow for a ratio of 5:1;
- when using all nylon (or mostly nylon), allow for a ratio of at least 7:1 – more if using a Danforth or other lightweight anchor, as these anchors rely not on their weight, but on a small angle of scope for holding power.

If you have the room, you should always let out more anchor rode if you are in doubt about how well the anchor is set or are expecting worsening conditions, such as an increase in wave height or wind velocity.

### Selecting an anchorage

When selecting an anchorage, the primary considerations are the type of sea bottom and the prevailing wind and wave conditions. And the novice sailor would be well advised to ask more experienced mariners about local anchorages.

A good anchorage is one that provides not only good shelter from large waves, but also good holding ground. No matter how well sheltered an area, an area with deep water and a rocky bottom will not be secure.

An ideal anchorage is one that is protected from the wind and seas from all directions. Coves that have breakwaters – either natural or man-made – are calm inside. Wave action against the boat will therefore not be an issue. However, if an anchorage is surrounded by low land, wind will still be a factor regardless of how well it is sheltered from the swell or large waves. Coral reefs, which serve well to block ocean swells, are so low as to provide little or no protection from prevailing winds. This is an important factor to consider, and the prudent skipper

would ensure that there is enough room to provide plenty of scope.

When anchoring in a river, be aware that the wind will play a role on the direction in which the vessels lay when at anchor. As important, perhaps more important, will be the current. Be sure to study how other vessels in the area are oriented, and be sure to determine exactly how the vessel will rest at its anchor before considering it secure.

The depth and shape of a vessel below the waterline may be an important factor. A large motorboat with a shallow draft may be more affected by wind conditions than a small sailboat with a full keel.

While most vessels in an anchorage tend to orient themselves in the same direction, current can play havoc with this rule. When anchoring in a river, be sure to anchor in such a way that your vessel does not come to rest in the main channel. This is especially important when anchoring in a tidal river, which can have currents shifting 180 degrees several times a day.

Another factor to consider when selecting an anchorage is the surrounding water depth. If the wind or current shifts while you are at anchor, thereby swinging the vessel in another direction, will the vessel come in contact with a submerged ledge? When leaving a vessel for any period of time, always ensure that there is ample water and protection in a full circle (360 degrees) around where the anchor is set.

### SETTING THE ANCHOR

If proceeding to an anchorage under sail, select the spot you want your boat to be in your mind's eye. Picture how it will be positioned in relation to other boats and the shore. Then communicate this plan to the person who will be lowering the anchor into the water; do this before she is positioned on the foredeck, and you won't have to yell. Be sure that she understands exactly where you plan to be, and be sure that you each understand how you will communicate with the other as you approach. You don't want the anchor to go down too soon, nor do you want it to go down too late; a set of hand signals may be necessary.

After you have rounded the boat into the wind, have the person on the foredeck strike the jib; this means that it will not be flogging around, threatening to knock her into the water, when she is attempting to

## Good scope

'Scope' is the ratio of rode length to water depth. The more rode you let out, the more scope you have.

When in doubt about the security of your anchorage, let out more scope, if there's room, to increase the holding power.

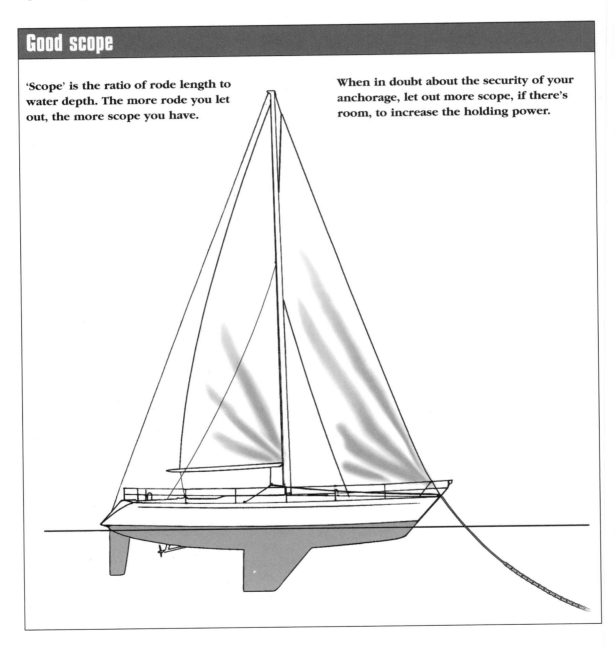

communicate with the helmsman or lowering the anchor.

Drop or lower the anchor only once the vessel has lost all its headway. The wind should then start to push the vessel astern. Ease out the rode slowly, maintaining tension on the anchor rode, either by holding it between your hands or by taking a turn around a cleat or bitt. This will keep the boat's bow into the wind and help set the anchor in the bottom.

Once an anchor is on the bottom and enough scope is released, it is necessary to fully 'set' the anchor. A forceful tug on the anchor rode, either by hand or by backing down under power or backing the sails, ensures the anchor's flukes will dig into the bottom. The idea is to impose a more significant load than you expect the boat will subjected to by the wind and waves during the time it will be anchored. Imagine the flukes digging into the mud or sand. How much force is necessary? More than you might think. Practice and judgement are the best tools for knowing your anchor will hold. Try practising by setting an anchor on shore, either a sandy beach or a grassy slope. Pull on the anchor. See the flukes dig? That's the idea. Never underestimate the power of the wind and waves.

## Anchoring options

The variability of the weather and topography means that it may be necessary to employ more than one style of anchoring to keep the vessel in the desired position. The most straightforward style is simply dropping the primary anchor and easing back on the anchor while paying out the recommended scope – as described above.

Occasionally it is necessary to let out more than one anchor. There are several ways to accomplish this. When dropping two anchors it is important not to let them tangle. If you drop them one on top of the other, or in the same line, they will definitely become entangled. The idea is to set the anchors in such a way as to form a 'Y'-shape with the boat, one anchor set at an angle off the port bow and the other off the starboard bow. To accomplish this, drop the first anchor, and, without setting it, steer the vessel to the point where you would like the second anchor to be deployed, the whole time paying out rode on the first, taking great care not to wrap the rode around your prop if under power. Drop the second anchor, then allow the vessel to drift back with the wind. You want to release the same amount of scope on each anchor rode, so that the load is equally divided.

## Bahamian style

If you expect your vessel to swing in the current, consider setting two anchors in the

Bahamian style: one anchor out in the direction of the current's two possible directions.

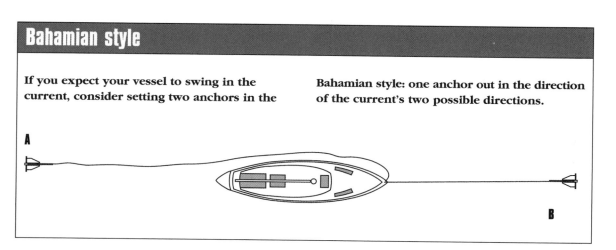

## Bahamian

When anchoring in an area where the current is expected to shift during the time that the vessel will be at anchor, you should drop the two anchors as described above, but allow the vessel to drift with the current while paying out the line. Once the second anchor is dropped, recover half the rode of the first. The vessel uses only one at anchor at a time, swinging with the current as the tide changes. If the current is very strong, recovering half the rode could be difficult without a good windlass, so consider setting the first and taking the second to its position in the dinghy.

## Med moor

So-called because of the Mediterranean custom of mooring stern-first to a dock, and boarding over the stern, the Med moor involves setting an anchor prior to backing toward a dock. The anchor will keep the bow from swinging into other vessels, and the stern is made off with two lines, which creates a stable triangle of mooring lines.

Drop the anchor as far out into the channel as required by the scope ratio – for example, in water that is 3m (10ft) deep and when using all-chain rode, you want 9m (30ft) of scope. Next, back into the dock, maintaining tension on the rode. Then throw stern lines ashore to be secured at an angle. Once close enough to the dock, take up the anchor rode to the point that the vessel is far enough to the dock that it will not bump, but close enough to use a gangway or minimize time in the dinghy.

## ANCHOR WATCH

How do you know that your vessel has remained in the position you left it and not dragged anchor? There are several ways to do this – for a complete discussion on the navigational aspects of maintaining an anchor watch, see Chapter 7. The most important is to maintain a situational awareness that allows you to be aware of any change. When an anchor drags, one can often hear a grinding noise, the sound of the anchor skipping across the bottom.

If you reach over and touch the rode, wrapping your hand around the line or chain, you can feel this most directly. Look around you, studying the relative position of

## Med moored

When Med moored, a vessel has an anchor off the bow (B) and is secured by the stern to the dock (A). This is the custom in many areas where there is a shortage on dock space, such as in many Mediterranean ports – hence the name.

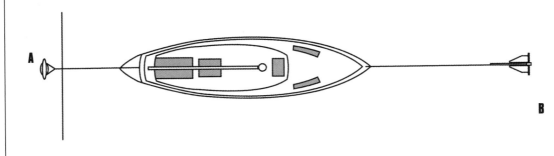

# Anchoring – a few tricks

Anchoring is not a strict science. With experience, each mariner will come up with ways that work with the equipment at hand and in the conditions he encounters. The best way to anchor is the way that works.

The following are a few tricks to make anchoring safer and more comfortable:

- In the event that there is not ample room in a given anchorage, use a sentinel to increase scope without paying out more line. Drop a weight down the rode to a point roughly halfway down its length, which will diminish the angle of the rode as it rises away from the anchor on the bottom. In effect, this also creates a sort of shock absorber for the vessel, the line only going taut when the greatest strain is imposed. It is possible to buy a purpose-built sentinel at a chandlery, replete with a sheave and retrieval line, but nearly any weight will do, including a spare anchor. Simply slide it down the rode in the same manner.

- Most boats will sail back and forth on their anchors in certain conditions. To prevent this, it is often helpful to drop a second anchor. This anchor should be dropped after the vessel is securely anchored on its primary anchor. Drop the second anchor straight down, accounting for the tide, to prevent the boat from sailing to and fro, and tugging all the while at the primary anchor. The anchor is a dead weight, not set in the traditional sense, but it should impose just enough force to keep the bow oriented into the wind.

your boat and other vessels or landmarks on shore. As discussed earlier, the best way to stop an anchor dragging is to slowly ease out more rode to increase the scope.

If this still does not help – if weather conditions are deteriorating, for example – it might be necessary to get under way and reset the anchor or select a more sheltered anchorage.

## MOORING
### Docking equipment

Each boat should have four lengths of line, three-strand or braided, and with an eye splice in one end. Nylon is a good choice, as it stretches when there is a load on the line, which is good for a docking line; you want there to be some elasticity to a line when the boat is lying alongside.

(Note that you don't want this same property for a halyard – the line that pulls up a sail – as you want the sail to remain fully up and tight in the position you first secured it.)

Each boat should have four fenders. Fenders should be secured to the stanchions, or lifelines, so that they are not touching the water's surface, but must also be positioned low enough that they will actually lie snugly between the hull and the dock. If a fender is too high or if there is significant wave action that causes the vessel to rise and fall while alongside, a fender will work itself free, allowing the hull to come in contact with the dock, scratching paint or damaging the hull itself.

Fenders should be secured around a stanchion or lifeline with two strong half-hitches; do not use a clove hitch, which will probably work itself free when there is a strain on the line.

### Alongside a dock

The most common way to moor a vessel is by securing it alongside a floating dock or fixed pier. When approaching a dock, first play out the entire manoeuvre in your mind. Consider the direction from which the wind is blowing and how strong it is. How many people are available to assist? Are there any on the dock to catch lines? Docking a vessel involves bringing large objects together in an environment that is always moving and always changing. Be sure that all your lines are ready, coiled, and affixed with a heaving line if necessary, and that all fenders are properly secured.

Let's assume, for an example, that you are preparing to land a 6-m (20-ft) sailboat with an inboard engine alongside a floating dock. You have one other crew member on board, as well as a person on the dock to handle your lines. Talk the manoeuvre through with the crew member.

It is helpful to number your lines. Most vessels will be secured with at least four lines: a bow line, which serves to go roughly straight across and a little ahead to the dock; an after-leading 'spring line', which will prevent your vessel from slipping forward when tied alongside; a forward-leading spring line, which prevents the vessel from slipping back when tied alongside; and a stern line, which goes straight across and a little aft to the dock. The bow and stern lines serve as 'breast lines', keeping the vessel snug against the dock. You might number these lines 1 through 4: 1 is the bow line; 2, the after-leading spring; 3, the forward-leading spring; and 4, the stern line.

The best way to manoeuvre a boat alongside is the easiest and most simple way that you can come up with for the given conditions. If there is no current and no wind, try sending the bow line across first, letting your propeller control the stern.

Similarly, if there is a breeze blowing off the dock, sending the bow line across to the person on the dock will let you have the bow secured before the wind catches it and forces it back away from the dock. The person at the helm can then pass the stern line across after the bow line is attached to the dock.

While there is no rule about whether the eye splice of a docking line should go to the dock or stay with the boat, take this tip from the shipping industry. If you affix the splice to your boat, casting the bitter end of the line to the dock hand, he will haul your boat in to where he thinks it should be. If you pass him the splice, you and your crew will control the tension of the line, meaning that your boat will come alongside in the manner you want. So, pass the splice-end to the person on the dock, point or verbalize to the cleat you would like to have the line secured to, then control the line's tension as you see fit. (However, if you're shorthanded, sailing alone, or with inexperienced crew, and you know that the person on the dock is skilled, you might prefer to let him have control.)

As always, secure your boat with 'fair leads' – in other words, with lines that are as untangled as possible. When you make the first turn around the cleat or bitt, imagine how it lies most securely. Imagine also how the next turn will lie in relation to it. If the line has to be crossed or is fouled, this is not a fair lead. Most cleats should be arranged on deck in a manner that allows a fair lead. Using a fair lead also ensures that the line can be released in a hurry if necessary.

After making the first turn around the cleat, make a figure-of-eight turn on each of the cleat's horns. Then apply a locking hitch by burying the bitter end of the line beneath the bight of the loop and pulling it tight. Using a single locking hitch is both secure and easy enough to free if you need to adjust lines in a hurry. Don't put a dozen figure-of-eight turns on the cleat followed by half a dozen locking hitches. A few turns and one locking hitch is enough.

## FENDERING

Whenever you approach a dock or another vessel with the intention of coming alongside, be sure to have ample fenders available and in the deployed position. Set your fenders up in advance, tying them to stanchions or cleats at a length that will do the most good. (If you're mooring alongside a low dock, make sure that the fenders are hung low enough so that they will be positioned between the hull and dock.)

Keep at least one fender free – a 'roving' fender to be used by a crew member whose role is to position the fender between the boat and dock in areas that may not be anticipated. Mooring alongside is tricky; if not executed perfectly, you will need this extra fender to be slipped into place. Having

a crew member be responsible for a roving fender is a good idea whenever you approach a dock or navigate your way through a mooring field, provided you have enough crew to spare to handle this task. Even if you don't, consider keeping one fender aside, not secured anywhere, so that a crew member can deploy it quickly in the event that it's needed.

Once your vessel is secured alongside with all lines in place, take another look at the fenders and be certain that they are in the most vulnerable areas. Remember that your vessel will have a different motion than the dock, especially if the dock is not floating, so adjust your fenders accordingly, being sure

## Bow roller

A bow roller reduces chafe on the anchor rode and eases the act of raising and lowering the anchor.

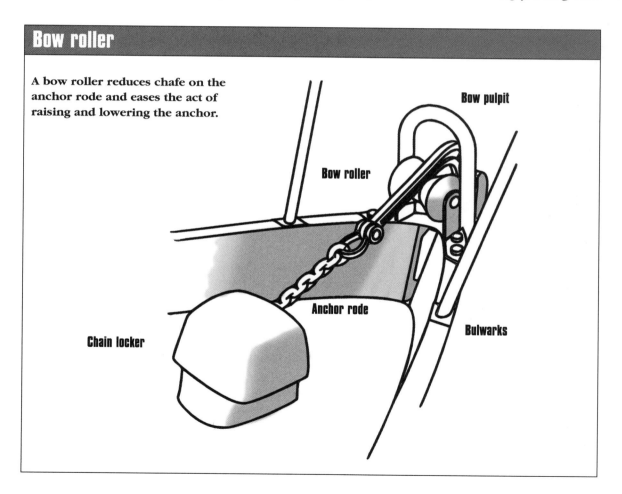

Bow pulpit

Bow roller

Anchor rode

Bulwarks

Chain locker

## Moored and anchored

In certain conditions, it may be necessary to set an anchor prior to lying alongside a dock. An anchor will help you to get under way when winds are setting you onto the dock, and it also helps to ease the strain of the boat against the dock. Always consider all options before leaving a boat alongside.

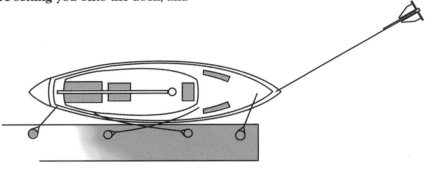

that a passing wake or the rise and fall of the tide will not work your fenders loose. If you leave your vessel for any period of time, be sure that it is in an area that is reasonably free of such motion. If it's not, consider anchoring or putting the vessel on a mooring.

### PICKING UP A MOORING

For a number of reasons, picking up a mooring is preferable to setting an anchor. First, it is less hassle to reach over the side, grab hold of a pennant and slip it over the post than it is to prepare an anchor, select an appropriate anchorage, and then go through the motions of setting and securing it. Secondly, it is easier to slip a mooring than to haul onboard an anchor that may be heavy and which is probably muddy from lying on the bottom.

If you pick up a mooring, make sure that the mooring anchor is heavy enough to handle your boat. If you pick up a private mooring, ask the owner or marina operator to tell you what's on the bottom. And because a mooring arrangement is only as secure as its weakest link, ask what type of chain and also exactly when it was last pulled from the water. If you plan on leaving your boat for any period of time, you may consider checking the mooring yourself by going into the water with a mask. If you don't feel secure about the mooring, don't leave your boat.

When approaching a mooring, have a crew member stand by on the bow with a boathook. Let that person direct you – either with hand signals or load commands – to the mooring. It may be necessary to back down your engine at the last moment so that you don't overshoot the mooring.

Once the mooring pennant is aboard, lead it into the boat using the fairest lead possible. How will it lead most directly and with the least amount of chafe over the side and into the water? That's how you want to lead the line.

Once passed over your Samson post or bow cleat, secure the heavy line with another spare line from your vessel. This will prevent the pennant working free.

## 'RAFTING' ALONGSIDE

If you are sailing in company with another vessel, consider 'rafting' together. One vessel proceeds to an anchorage, then drops and secures its anchor. The second vessel comes alongside, as if approaching a dock. If conditions are calm enough, you won't need another anchor set; you can both hang off the one anchor. Plus, provided there is enough scope to account for the weight and windage of the second vessel, hanging off a single anchor prevents the possibility of two sets of ground tackle being tangled.

Another advantage to rafting – besides the social aspect – is that two boats rafted together take up less room in an anchorage (or mooring field). If an anchorage is tight, offering enough room for only one more vessel, two boats rafted together will conserve space. Take extra care when securing lines and fenders between rafted vessels, and always use extreme caution when stepping between the two. Because rafted vessels are vulnerable to the wind and waves, do not leave them unattended except in the calmest of conditions.

## Approaching the dock

In figure A, the boat is being set onto the dock by the wind. It may be necessary to back the engine down as you make the final approach, allowing the wind to push your boat against the dock.

With the wind coming off the dock, B, your approach needs to be made more aggressively, since the wind will force your bow away. It is crucial to keep up just enough speed for steerageway in this scenario.

With the wind coming parallel to the dock, C, docking is the simplest of all, since it will help keep the vessel aligned with the dock, provided you don't let the wind catch the bow and push it away from the dock.

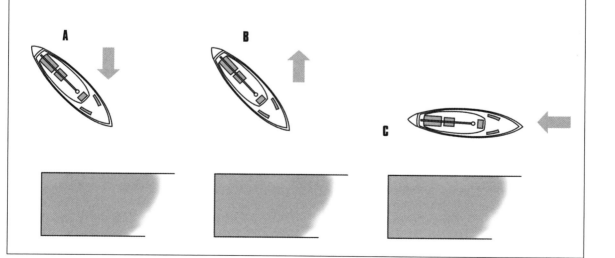

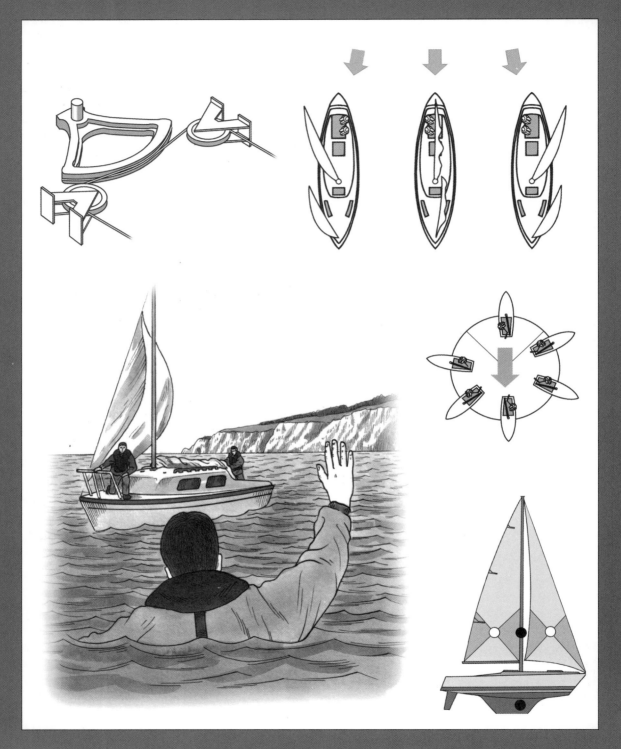

# CHAPTER 7

# The mechanics of steering and sailing

For thousands of years, people have harnessed the wind to transport themselves across the water. Whether for business or pleasure, the principle is the same – transferring the force and direction of the wind into sails that are trimmed to rush the vessel on its desired course.

A common misconception is that a sailboat is pushed through the water by the wind. Actually, it is pulled – by a force that has come to be known as the Bernoulli effect, after the Swiss scientist Daniel Bernoulli (1700–82) who discovered exactly how this effect worked. A gull's wing, an aeroplane's wing, and a sail – all are air foils. The cross section of a foil shows a rounded, tear-shaped side that is complemented by a flatter, or concave, side. When air moves across this shape, a low-pressure system is

## Low-pressure lift

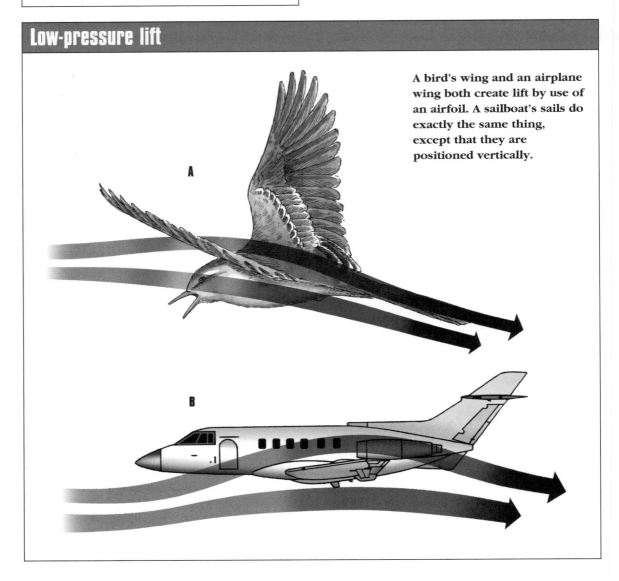

A bird's wing and an airplane wing both create lift by use of an airfoil. A sailboat's sails do exactly the same thing, except that they are positioned vertically.

created on the rounded side of the foil because the air moves faster across that side. In the case of the sail, this is the back, known as the 'leaward side'. The vacuum created by the low pressure then pulls on the back of the sail. This force draws at an angle of 45 degrees to the back side of the sail. The keel and rudder of a sailboat counteract the lateral component of this force, leaving the forward component to drive the boat in the desired direction.

In the case of the airplane, the low-pressure system created on the top of the wings – which is caused by the rushing of air as the plane speeds down the runway – draws the plane upwards at the same angle.

The rudder serves the same directional purpose on an airplane as on a boat, but the job of the boat's keel is done by gravity in the case of an airplane.

The luff, or forward section, of the sail is where the force is centred, so sailors need to pay most attention to this area, being sure it remains full and drawing. If it is flapping, or 'luffing', the sail is not drawing the vessel efficiently and needs to be trimmed – that is, brought in until the sail is full. If the sail is brought in too tightly, the foil shape is not being properly utilized. If you know the direction of the wind, it is a simple matter to keep the foil angled properly by adjusting the sail itself.

## CENTRE OF EFFORT

A boat's centre of effort is the point at which the wind's force is centred on a boat's sails. Imagine the wind on the centre of effort as a giant finger pushing on the boat's sails. If the finger pushes the sails near the bow, the bow will turn away; if pushed near the stern, the stern will be pushed away. The sail area's centre of effort is that magic position that is neither too far forward nor too far aft. A boat's sail area is designed to have its centre of effort positioned so that the act of steering is made as easy as possible. You do not want the rudder to be fighting the sails; you want both the rudder and sails to be balanced, to work together to move the vessel on a straight course.

Each sail has its own centre of effort. When combined, a single centre of effort for the boat's entire sail area is determined. Most boats are designed to have the vessel's centre of effort be perfectly balanced over the boat's 'centre of lateral resistance' – that is, the point on the boat's underbody that is the pivot point. If the centre of effort is positioned directly over the boat's centre of lateral resistance, the boat will be steered with a minimal of effort by the helmsman.

Some vessels are designed with 'weather helm', which means that the centre of effort is positioned slightly aft of the centre of lateral resistance so that, when the helm is not being tended, the boat will round up into the wind and stall. Hence the term 'weather helm', which means the tendency of a boat to turn to weather. This is often a helpful feature, particularly for solo sailors: if a single-handed helmsman is knocked overboard, he will be able to swim back to his boat (as opposed to watching it sail away on a straight course without him).

## SAIL TRIM

A sailboat has its sails trimmed on one 'tack' or another, either port or starboard. If the wind is coming across the vessel's starboard side, causing the sails to be filled on the opposite side, the vessel is on a starboard tack. If the wind is coming across the port side, it is on a port tack, despite the fact that the sails are trimmed to starboard. Make sense? Just think of the wind in relation to the boat. The side over which the wind is blowing is the tack that the boat is on. (Note that the noun 'tack' is not to be confused with the verb 'to tack', which involves turning the vessel through the wind – see below.)

To 'trim' a boat's sail is to adjust the angle of the sail in relation to the wind direction. Remember that a sail is a foil, which needs to be directed into the wind to function properly, creating maximum lift on the leading edge. If a boat has more than one sail, it is crucial to keep all the sails properly trimmed each time the boat's course is changed.

## POINTS OF SAIL

A sail cannot simply be raised and the boat turned on the desired course – that would be too easy. Nor can a sailboat sail directly into the wind. The mariner needs to know from which direction the wind is blowing and adjust the sails accordingly. Wind direction is measured on the compass, using either the named direction (north or east, for example) or, more precisely, any point from 001 degrees to 360 degrees. The idea is always to trim the sails for maximum efficiency – the trim changes with the boat's orientation to the wind. The sails work at their most efficient only when they are trimmed at a given angle in relation to the wind. Because the wind can blow from any direction on the compass, we need to be vigilant with trimming sails. For simplicity, the 'points of sail' – the angle at which the sails are trimmed in relation to the boat – are described below in just five categories: a close haul, close reach, beam reach, broad reach, and run.

## Centre of effort

Each sailboat has a centre of effort – the position that is the combined lateral force on the sails – and a centre of lateral resistance, which is the force resisted by the keel. These two forces balance each other: lift moves the boat forward, steered by the rudder.

## 1. Close haul (or beating)

Every boat differs slightly in the angle at which it can be pointed into the wind and still keep its sails full. High-tech, round-the-buoy race boats such as America's Cup competitors point higher – that is, they can nose closer to the direction of the wind and still have their sails full – than, say, a nineteenth-century square-rigger designed to sail in the tradewinds. Boats today typically point between 30 degrees and as much as 70 degrees to the wind, depending on their intended use.

Sailing as close as one can to the wind and still have the sails full and drawing – a manoeuvre that is called 'full and by' in the parlance of traditional sailing ships – is to sail close hauled. If the desired course is upwind of the boat's location, a series of 'tacks' will be necessary to bring the vessel to that location.

## 2. Close reach

To sail on a close reach is to have the wind coming over the bow as when sailing close hauled, but not as tight. The term 'reach' means to let the sails out a bit, the degree being defined by the direction of the wind in relation to the boat – close, beam, or broad.

## 3. Beam reach

When the wind is coming at an angle perpendicular to the heading of the boat, the vessel is on a beam reach. For maximum efficiency, the sails are eased, not sheeted in tight as on a close reach. If the sails are too flat, the wind will hit them broadside, and, although this will keep them full, the force will be more sideways than forward, and the boat will make less speed and more 'leeway'.

## 4. Broad reach

When the vessel is moving with the wind coming over its 'quarter' – from abaft the

## Points of sail

A vessel pointed directly into the wind (position 1) is considered to be 'in irons' and will not move forward. A vessel in position 2 is close hauled or 'beating.' In position 3, a boat is on a broad reach, and, in position 4, it is 'running', with the wind over the stern. A boat in position 5 is back to a broad reach reach (wind over quarter), while in position 6 it is on a beam reach.

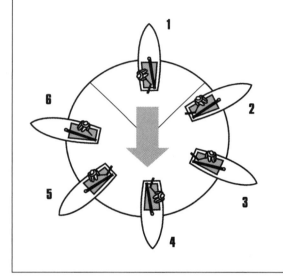

## LEEWAY

Leeway is the unintended direction a vessel moves sideways through the water away from the course intended by helmsman. One can often see leeway occurring in one's wake; if the wake is straight, there is no leeway through the water.

If the wake curves away to windward, the vessel is making leeway for some reason, either because the vessel is being steered too close to the wind in an inefficient manner or because the sails are improperly trimmed.

## WIND DIRECTION AND FORCE

Long before it is time to raise a vessel's sails, the prudent mariner will know the direction of the wind. There are many clues available. If the vessel is at a mooring, it will probably be lying with its bow into the wind (unless the current is - unhelpfully - proving more forceful than the wind). If a vessel is equipped with telltales or pennants of any kind, these will also indicate the direction of the wind. It is imperative to know the wind's direction prior to putting up sail, as you do not want the sails to be filled until you are ready to start moving.

You should also have a sense of the wind's force. This can be determined in a variety of ways, either by using an anemometer (mounted on the vessel or handheld) or by studying the surface of the water to determine the force on the Beaufort Scale (see Chapter 1). If the wind is blowing too strong for the vessel's full rig, you should put a reef in the sail - in other words, reduce the sail area - before getting under way.

### True wind versus apparent wind

If you are standing on a dock and the wind is blowing at 20 knots from the east across your face, you are feeling the effects of the true wind, both in terms of its force and its direction. As soon as you start to move, you introduce your own motion - the speed and direction in which you are travelling - into

beam - the vessel is on a broad reach. Sails are eased even more than when on a beam reach.

## 5. Run

A vessel that is running downwind has its sails eased as far out as is practical, often against the shrouds. A vessel's jib will often be blanketed by the mainsail, causing the sail to flap uselessly. This is okay; the jib cannot get clean air because the mainsail is blocking the wind.

If it is possible to manoeuvre the jib to the opposite side of the boat from the main and be kept full, the vessel is said to be sailing 'wing-and-wing'.

the equation, and this results in the 'apparent wind' — the wind that you feel when you are in motion.

If you were riding a motorboat at 10 knots, straight into the 20-knot easterly wind that you had felt on your face at the dock, you would feel 30 knots of apparent wind on your face. If you turned the boat around and headed west, you would feel only 10 knots of wind – and you would be feeling it on your back as the true wind speed is 20 knots, twice the speed that you are making in your boat.

The difference between true wind and apparent wind is especially noticeable on a sailboat when you change from, say, being close hauled to being on a broad reach. You may feel the wind whipping in your face on the close haul, only to find yourself wondering where the wind went once you slacked off the sheets and started moving with the direction of the wind. The wind hasn't died; you've just combined your course and speed with the wind's, thereby diminishing the apparent wind force.

Sailing involves moving a boat through the water in numerous angles relative to the wind, so it is not often easy to determine the exact apparent wind. If we know the wind's true direction and force, we can figure out precisely the apparent wind by drawing out a vector diagram. Such a calculation is not necessary, but an awareness of the difference definitely makes for a more educated sailor.

## TACKING (OR COMING ABOUT)

You have set the sails, taken off from the mooring, and are sailing along at a good clip, the wind in your hair and a smile on your face. Sooner or later, though, you're going to have to change direction, particularly if you are trying to get somewhere that is upwind of your location. If you're attempting this, you will have started out close hauled, with the sheets in tight and paying careful attention not to luff the sails. You will have steered the boat as close to the wind as possible to make progress upwind.

To tack the boat is to turn the rudder to bring the bow through the eye of the wind. The sails will fill on the opposite side, and, if the sails are trimmed at the same relative angle as they were on the opposite tack, the boat will continue on its new course at the same angle to the wind.

## GYBING A VESSEL

If you are on a broad reach or a run and you want to change direction to a point that would cause your sails to move from one side of the boat to the other, you need to execute a gybe. Gybing and tacking have the same result – putting the boat on the opposite tack –

## How lift works

When the wind strikes the sail it splits and creates lift. The vessel moves ahead through the water when the lift is straightened by the keel into forward motion.

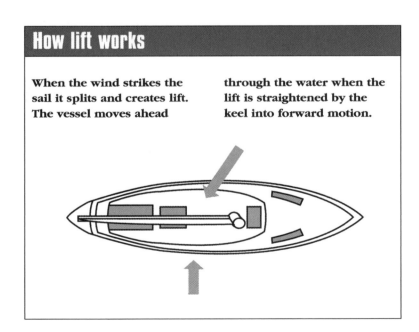

## Tacking

To tack, push the tiller away from the direction of wind. This will turn the bow into the wind, and the sails will 'luff'. Keep the tiller over until the bow is through the wind and the sails fill on the opposite side. Then straighten out the tiller and steady up on your new course.

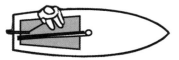  

but the manoeuvres differ. To tack involves moving the bow through the wind and crossing the sails; to gybe involves moving the stern through the eye of the wind.

Gybing is typically trickier than tacking, usually because if you choose to gybe you are probably proceeding on a broad reach or a run, which means that your sails are well eased. If you simply put the helm over to change course - as is the case with tacking - the sails would come across at a terrific rate, the sheets clearing the decks and threatening to sweep anything, and anyone, over the side. If a gybe is to be executed, make sure that the sheets are brought in before the helm is put over.

This means that the line, which will go slack momentarily as the sail crosses to the other side, is not allowed to tangle anything in its path - whether cleats, winches, or people's heads.

### HEADING UP; FALLING OFF

To turn the boat into the wind's direction is to 'head up'. To turn the boat away from the wind's direction is to 'fall off'. Sailing a boat on a desired course involves countless acts of heading up and falling off, as the watchful helmsman must always be attentive to the effect of the waves and variability of the wind on the boat.

If you head up too far, the sails luff; if the boat continues to head up until the bow passes through the wind, the sails will fill on the opposite side - for better (if you intended to tack) or worse (you weren't paying proper attention). If you fall off too far, the boat will eventually gybe - that is, the stern will pass through the eye of the wind.

## Port tack

A vessel is on a port tack, as shown, when the wind is coming over the port side.

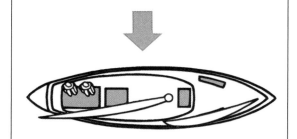

## REEFING

To reef a sail is to temporarily reduce its overall area. The idea is to lower the boat's centre of effort so that the force of the wind continues to create lift without creating too much heel. This is accomplished by rolling up the sail from the bottom, using the 'reef points' to tie it off. To do so, use the 'reef knot' – called a square knot ashore – being careful to tie the reef points all on the same side of the sail. This makes the process consistent and is easier to shake out when the wind becomes lighter.

If you are reefing before getting under way, raise the sail only part way, being sure to stop hauling the sail up when the reef points are at a position as to be accessible. Most sails are equipped with an outhaul, which allows the new clew to be hauled both aft and down, drawing the sail tight. It is then time to secure the new clew and tack.

Using spare line, tie the new clew securely around the boom. (Use a patch of canvas to prevent chafe between the spare line and the sail.) Use another length of line to secure the new tack of the sail to the boom. Many boats are equipped with a pennant and hook, which should be clipped into the new tack's grommet.

Then tie off the reef points by first tucking them under the foot of the sail. Do not tie them around the boom, even if the reef points are long enough. You want the reduced sail to have the same foil shape as when it's fully set.

Once the reef points are secure, the new tack and clew tightly lashed, it is safe to set the sail normally. You will notice that the diminished sail area enhances the boat's ability to sail safely in strong wind.

### When to reef

How do you know when it's time to reef? Every boat is different, and you need to know your boat's limits, but the rule of thumb is that it is typically time to reef when the thought first occurs to you. Many people put off the act of reefing until the vessel is already overpowered, which is both a dangerous and uncomfortable situation. You don't want to be sailing at a severe angle of heel. It is inefficient and potentially dangerous.

If you have a chance to reef a sail when the vessel is still alongside a dock or on a mooring, this is the best time. The crew are then able to concentrate on the task at hand without also worrying about trying to steer a boat while the sails are flapping uselessly, to manoeuvre around traffic, or to keep a lookout. Remember, it is always easier to shake out a reef once you are under way than it is to put one in.

Knowing how to reef your boat is essential. Even if you put in a reef in conditions that are mild, only to shake it out afterward, you will be practising a skill that will keep you safe in future. If the wind has increased beyond your boat's full-sail limits, putting in a reef may be a hassle, but this will be far outweighed by the relief when the vessel begins to move more comfortably – and safely.

## Starboard tack

**A vessel is on a starboard tack when the wind is coming over the starboard side.**

## Performing a tack

To tack a boat, turn the vessel up into the wind (A). The sails will flap, and the boat will slow (B). Keep the tiller over until the boat is through the wind and the sails fill on the opposite side (C). Release the jib sheet that was being used, and take up on the jib sheet on the opposite side.

C

B

A

Should you shake out a reef when your sailing is finished for the day? Not necessarily. The following day could also bring strong winds, which will mean that you'll thank yourself for leaving it in the night before. If not, take a few seconds to shake out the reef and raise your full sail.

### HEAVING TO

It is sometimes necessary to pause while under way, to take stock of a situation or simply to get some rest from steering and line handling. The best way to do this is to 'heave to'. This means adjusting the sails and configuring the rudder in such a way that it

## Performing a gybe

To gybe a boat, which means to turn the boat so that the stern passes through the eye of the wind, tighten the sails in preparation for the gybe, then turn the tiller in the desired direction. The sails will snap across quickly as the boat turns. Ease out the sails once your boat is safely through the gybe.

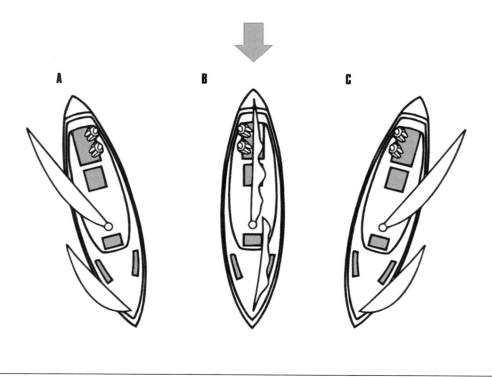

A        B        C

will bring the vessel to a stop or to a very slow, sideways crawl.

Assuming that you are sailing a sloop, which has both a mainsail and jib, heaving to is straightforward and fun to execute. If you are on a port tack, head up into the wind as though performing a tack. Allow the jib to fill on the starboard side, but don't cross the sheet; simply keep it made off to the cleat, and the jib will remain back-winded to starboard. Once through the tack, put the rudder hard to starboard. This configuration of the rudder will result in the boat wanting to head up; however, the backed jib should prevent the vessel from actually coming about. With the rudder hard over and the jib backed, the vessel will perform a sideways, scalloping motion through the water and not make much headway.

With a little practice and fiddling, most boats can be made to heave to, a practice that gives the mariner a chance to catch his breath or attend to other, possibly urgent, tasks.

## Rudder and tiller

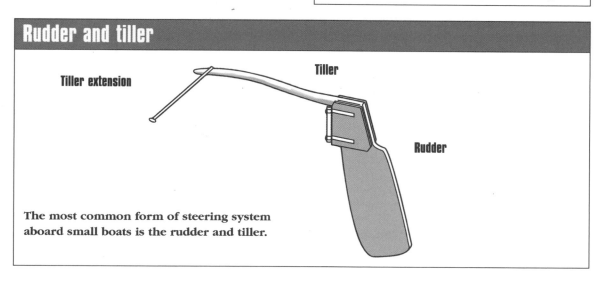

Tiller extension

Tiller

Rudder

The most common form of steering system aboard small boats is the rudder and tiller.

## Communication on board

It is imperative that the crew be kept informed of the manoeuvres the helmsman is planning. Crew can help trim the sails, ease the sheets, adjust the vang, or keep a lookout. All crew should communicate with each other constantly. Before coming about, it is a custom for the helmsman to announce his intention. 'Ready about!', spoken loudly and clearly, informs the crew that he is preparing to come about. Crew should respond in kind, 'Ready!', then stand by on the sheets and lower their heads because the boom will soon be coming across. Once the helmsman puts the tiller or helm over, he announces, 'Helm's alee!' This informs the crew that the vessel has entered its tack.

When the helmsman is interested in gybing the boat, he announces, 'Prepare to gybe!' Once the crew have responded with 'Ready!' and are at their stations, the helm is put over, and the helmsman announces, 'Gybe ho!', informing the crew that the sails are, at that instant, coming across. In the interests of safety, it is crucial that the helmsman watches the sails carefully when preparing for a gybe.

If an order is given, it is helpful that the person receiving the order should then repeat it so that the helmsman knows that he has been heard. For example, if a helmsman is preparing to anchor and has already informed the crew of his intentions – shown the crew on the chart where he would like to anchor, how the sails should come down, and when the anchor should be prepared – he might then say, 'Stand by the anchor.' If the person on the foredeck misheard, thinking that he was being asked to drop the anchor at that moment instead of stand by, the helmsman would hear in response, 'Drop the anchor.' He could then repeat his instruction to stand by the anchor.

Such procedure is especially important when sailing at night or in rough weather. Indeed, it is standard practice aboard the world's merchant ships. Using this procedure at all times, no matter how mild the present conditions may be, prepares the crew for those times when such clarity could make all the difference.

# MAN OVERBOARD!

Every year, people fall from boats into the water and drown. Despite massive efforts by coastguard agencies around the world to persuade people to wear life jackets at all times, the overwhelming majority of people who fall in the water and drown are not wearing life jackets. Always wear a life jacket when sailing or rowing a small boat.

This may sound oversimplistic, but the most important way to avoid a man-overboard drill is to prevent someone falling overboard. Always remember that the rail of a boat is, for all intents and purposes, the edge of the world. When someone enters the water accidentally, a series of well-rehearsed manoeuvres can be performed by the crew left on board to recover that person, but a man-overboard scenario is always potentially difficult, being dependent as it is on variable conditions on the water.

## When under power

Deploy a lifebuoy immediately. One crew member should be detailed to keep sight of the person overboard. If equipped with an engine, drop sails and start the motor. When approaching a person in the water under power, remember that a boat is powered by a propeller, a sharp, metal object that can inflect a fatal wound on someone who is in the water near the stern of the boat. Always take the engine out of gear, and consider shutting it down entirely when making the final approach to a person in the water. This will prevent the engine being accidentally engaged and therefore causing further harm to the person.

## Under sail

The best way to begin recovery of a person in the water is to stop the boat. This can be accomplished in a variety of ways. The quickest way to stop the boat is to head into the wind. This luffs the sails, preventing them from propelling the boat further, and is known as putting the boat 'in irons'. If the person in the water has already drifted far astern, bring the boat back to the person in the water.

If heading upwind, tack immediately with beam reach until you have room to gybe and close reach back to a position just to windward of the MOB, using the mainsheet and jib sheet to make a slow controlled approach. Stop the boat just to windward and drift downwind until recovery is possible. Heave to if necessary.

If you are heading downwind, harden on to a broad reach until you have room to tack, then close reach back to a position just to windward of the MOB. Stop the boat just to windward and drift downwind until recovery is possible.

All sailors should practice these manouvres until perfect using a bucket with a fender tied to it as your MOB.

# DINGHY USE

A wise man once said that a dinghy can make a fool of even the most experienced shipmaster. Knowing how to handle a small boat under oars is basic seamanship, but it is not to be underestimated.

It is important to keep one's centre of gravity low when moving around a dinghy. When stepping into a dinghy, always crouch, placing your foot in the centre of the bottom of the boat to prevent it upsetting.

When leaving a dinghy, be sure to remove the oars from the oarlocks, and stow them in the bottom of the boat. Then stow the oarlocks themselves, removing them from the upright position. This is especially important when bringing a dinghy alongside a dock or another boat, as the oarlocks can easily scratch or puncture a fine, painted finish. Stowing the oarlock also removes the possibility of having someone trip over them when moving from the dinghy to the dock or the other boat. Stowing the oars and oarlocks should be standard practice.

# Man overboard

When a person goes overboard, proceed to his location carefully so as not to injure him. You may need to douse the sails entirely and start the engine – if the boat is so equipped – or reduce sail to reduce speed. Here, the skipper has struck the mainsail and kept the jib up to make a slow approach.

# Telltales

'Telltales' are little strips of light cloth affixed to both sides of the sail and are helpful indicators. A helmsman trying to maintain a course on a close reach trims the sails accordingly – pulling them in as close as possible without allowing the sails to become too flat and lose their foil shape – then vigilantly watches the telltales to ensure the sails are drawing most efficiently. Telltales should lie flat against the sails, streaming aft at the same angle. If they aren't – if one telltale is pointing down and the other lying flat or dancing around – this is a sign that sails need trimming or the course needs to be adjusted.

This isn't to say that a helmsman steering a boat without telltales is lost. Quite the opposite. Telltales were invented for use by the pleasure boater; in the days before telltales, a mariner relied on her ability to read the wind as it moved across the waves and to feel the direction of the wind on her face, typically by pointing her nose into the wind and turning her head back and forth until the wind was blowing across her ears equally, which meant that her nose was pointed directly into the wind – the 'apparent wind' anyway.

**Trimmed correctly**

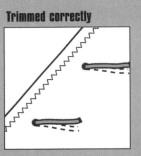

**Trim sheets in**

**Trim sheets out**

When approaching another boat or dock, it is crucial to keep your hands and fingers from coming between the two objects. You can use your hand to fend off or to grab hold of the dock or other boat, but be sure that your hand is never placed between the two objects. Even on a calm day, the wake of a passing boat could cause the dinghy to lurch violently against the dock, crushing anything in its path.

When towing a dinghy, be sure to make off the painter - the line attached to the dinghy's bow - securely to the stern of the sailboat. (Be sure to make the line off with a fair lead, which will make untying the line easier.) Adjust the length of the painter so that the dinghy will ride at a comfortable distance astern of the sailboat. If there are any waves, you should adjust the painter to the length of the wave interval so that the dinghy and sailboat ride the waves together: when the sailboat is on a crest, the dinghy should be on a crest; and, when the sailboat is in a trough, the dinghy should be in the trough. Adjusting the length of the line in this manner will make the towing free of an unpleasant jerking motion.

In heavy weather, the dinghy could become waterlogged and snap its painter. If possible, bring them onboard, and tether them upside down on the foredeck.

## Landing on a beach

Dinghies make excellent transportation between a sailboat and a beach. If tide is a concern, always account for the stage of the tide. Is it rising? If so, haul the dinghy up farther than you would if the tide is falling.

If leaving the dinghy for any period of time, always be sure to pull the dinghy up above the high-tide line. And always – no matter if there is no tidal change, you are leaving it for just a minute, or you cannot imagine a scenario in which your dinghy could wander off – tie your dinghy to an immovable object, whether tree, post, or suitably-shaped rock.

## MAINTENANCE
### Seacocks

A seacock, also known as a through-hull valve or simply a through hull, is a bronze valve that is affixed to the hull so that water, or other fluids, can be pumped in or out. Each valve should have its own designated wooden plug, tied to the valve for use in an emergency. Seacocks are part of every system that exchanges water with the outside of the boat – whether a marine toilet using salt water to flush, a sink that uses salt water or is pumped overboard, or the raw-water system on an engine's cooling system. (Sometimes, a boat is fitted with a manifold, which reduces the number of through-hull fittings.)

You should know where each through-hull fitting is located in the boat. In the event of a catastrophic leak, when you're hunting to find how water is entering the hull, you will want to check the integrity of the through-hull valve. If you want to avoid this frenzy altogether – wondering where each seacock is located and hoping that you've remembered them all – draw a schematic of your boat and indicate where each such valve is located.

The other reason for knowing the location of each seacock is so that they can each be serviced. When the boat is out of the water,

detach the clamps and hose from each valve, and disassemble the valves. Clean the valve thoroughly, then apply heavy-duty water-proof grease, working the grease into the valve assembly. Reinstall the valve. Always use two hose clamps on all through-hull fittings below the waterline. This is standard practice and assumes that at least one hose clamp will remain attached even if the other fails, perhaps as a result of corrosion.

## Marine toilet

A boat's head is a vulnerable piece of equipment. Every attempt should be made to ensure that all crew members and guests appreciate this fact and know not to attempt to flush anything other than toilet paper. Some vessel skippers even post a sign to this effect: 'Put nothing into the head unless you have eaten it first!'

Aside from treating a head gently, it is advisable to drop a tablespoonful of vegetable oil into the bowl regularly – once a week, for example. The oil helps to keep the rubber valves supple, maintaining the necessary tight seal.

Always flush a saltwater head with fresh water at the end of the boating season, being sure to completely drain the system after you have done so. If you live in an area that experiences freezing temperatures, flush the entire system with antifreeze.

## Standing rigging

The standing rigging of a boat is subject to all the forces imposed by the unforgiving marine environment, but it is often taken for granted and therefore overlooked in maintenance inspections.

Most rigs are constructed from stainless steel, and this can fail over time. Small structural cracks can appear on bolts, flanges, tangs, and turnbuckles (also called bottlescrews), making routine visual inspection essential. At the start of each boating season, when it comes time to step

## Cable and quadrant

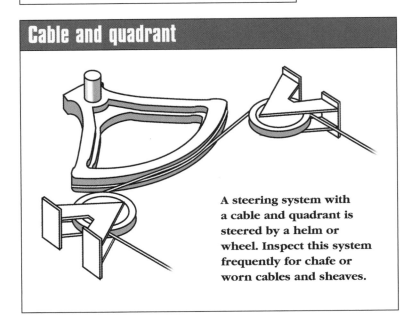

A steering system with a cable and quadrant is steered by a helm or wheel. Inspect this system frequently for chafe or worn cables and sheaves.

your mast and tune the rig, run each section of the rig through your fingers. 'Meathooks' in the wire – small barbs of hooklike wire that stand away from the rest of the strand – indicate that the wire cable has reached the end of its useful life. Not only is this unpleasant to handle, but it is also weak.

Cotter pins, clevis pins, and other small bits of hardware that need to be bent into shape to secure the rig should be replaced every season. Metal that is bent and twisted repeatedly becomes fatigued and weak. During the boating season, you should check all the components regularly, going up in the 'bosun's chair' if this can be done safely. If you tape your hardware with plastic tubing or perhaps electrical tape – to prevent your sails and running rigging from being torn on them – take off the tape at least once every year to inspect the attachment hardware.

### Running rigging

Inspect all the halyards and sheets – all lines on your boat – for signs of wear. Consider ways to lessen the possibility that a line will chafe in the same spot repeatedly. Most line is now constructed of man-made fabrics that are intended to resist the elements (salt water and ultraviolet (UV) rays, in particular). Even so, take care of your lines and they will serve your boat well, possibly for many years.

If a line is dirty – dragged through the mud, for example – take the time to rinse it until it is clean; small particles of sand and gravel will cut through the fibres of the rope. If a line looks worn, its colour has faded, and it has a fuzzy appearance, it is not as strong and resistant to stretch as when it was new. Replace it.

If the line is made of twisted strands, open the strands so that you can inspect the inside of the rope. If the rope has lost its roundness, it has worn a vee-shaped groove, and bits of fibre are coming away from the rope, replace the line. Line that is in good shape feels good in the hands, supple and smooth to the touch. If a line feels stiff and tangles easily when you try to coil it, you need to replace it.

### WINTERISING

As if the marine environment were not punishing enough, winter is harsher still. The vessel owner needs to guard against freezing temperatures in advance. If your boat is subjected to freezing temperatures in the off-season, you will need to be sure that all systems are drained of fresh water. Nontoxic antifreeze – propylene glycol – works well, provided it has not been diluted in water. When mixed with water, it will freeze like water.

## Worm gear

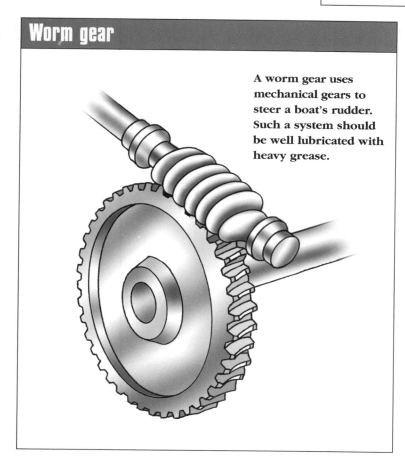

A worm gear uses mechanical gears to steer a boat's rudder. Such a system should be well lubricated with heavy grease.

been reached. In spring, drain the vodka into the bilge or pump it directly overboard. If your boat has a bilge plug, remove the plug when the boat is out of the water so that any water that has accumulated in the bilge can drain free.

Change all the engine's lubricating oil and transmission oil – and all attendant filters – at the end of each season. Lastly, you need to 'fog' the engine lightly with silicone spray.

Cover the boat, either with heavy canvas tarps or plastic sheeting, to keep off any unwanted rain and snow, and protect the boat's deck from months of wind-blown dust and damaging UV rays. Be sure that any boat covering is well ventilated. Stagnant air will contain moisture, initiating rotting.

The raw water cooling system on an inboard engine should be flushed with fresh water – if your boat is used in salt water – then run through with antifreeze. Replace the raw-water pump's impeller at the start of each boating season, coating it first with a layer of lithium grease.

Drain your boat's freshwater system and then pour in a gallon of inexpensive vodka, being sure that the freshwater pump has

### Sail storage

Remove the sails from the boat. Wash them in fresh water and allow them to dry thoroughly before folding them and placing them in storage.

It is a good idea to keep the sails packed in mothballs and stored in a dry, ventilated area to protect against mildew, insects, and vermin, which will reduce a suit of fine sails to tatters in a few short months.

# CHAPTER 8

# Navigation

**To master the art of navigation, you need first to have a firm grasp of its science. Navigation involves learning basic vector diagrams for making good position 'fixes'; the adding and subtracting of figures to determine true direction from compass direction; and the careful observation of your progress through the water – all to be performed with a tidiness that should satisfy the most severe schoolmistress.**

The best navigators are not mathematicians, however; they are people with sound judgement. Indeed, the art of navigation is the ability to call on one's skills at a time of need. Good judgement (and the Nautical Rules) tells us that we are never to rely on one single means of navigation, whether radar set or GPS, or one single aid to navigation, whether buoy or lighthouse, for establishing where we are at any time. One should always use one system to cross-check the other. Redundancy, double-checking, listening to that inner voice – these are all practices that make good navigators.

A navigator should take careful notes, keeping a log of the weather, the velocity and direction of the wind, and the position of the vessel at regular intervals.

## LATITUDE AND LONGITUDE
To find our way around the globe, we have set up a grid system that envelops the earth:

- Latitude lines, also called the Parallels, are the lines that lie horizontally, measured north and south of the equator. The equator itself is the central line of latitude – or 0 degrees. Lines of latitude progress north- and southward to 90 degrees, at which points are the earth's poles.

- Longitude lines run perpendicular to latitude. Longitude lines are not parallel, as they meet at the North and South poles. They are measured from 000 degrees to 180 degrees east and west of the Greenwich Meridian. Also called the Prime Meridian, this runs north and south on a line that passes through Greenwich, England. The line where east and west longitude meet is called the International Date Line, which runs north and south through the middle of the Pacific Ocean.

The Greenwich Meridian has not always been recognized internationally. Many of the countries of Europe, notably France and Spain, used their own central meridian for much of the past several hundred years, adopting the English system only in the late nineteenth century. In fact, the French attempted to establish the metric system for nautical measurement, which would have required using a compass with 400 grades, instead of 360 degrees.

Latitude and longitude are measured in degrees (°), minutes ('), and tenths of minutes. One degree of latitude is equal to 60 nautical miles, which is 6072 feet. (A statute mile is 5280 feet.) One minute of latitude is equal to one nautical mile.

The same cannot be said for longitude. As lines of longitude come together as they progress north or south, degrees of longitude are equivalent to 60 miles only at the equator. For this reason, one always measures distance from the left or right of the chart, which is where the latitude measurements are indicated. Longitude lines are measured along the tops and bottoms of charts.

When reading the latitude and longitude on charts, always determine which direction the numbers are progressing. In the Southern

## Latitude and longitude

**The globe is divided in a grid system, latitude for north–south measurement and longitude for east–west measurement.**

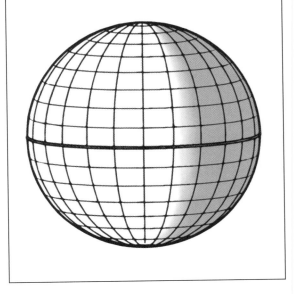

Hemisphere, latitude increases from top to bottom on the chart; in the Northern Hemisphere, it increases from bottom to top. If you are navigating off the west coast of South America (Southern Hemisphere, West Longitude), for example, the latitude on your chart will increase from top to bottom, and the longitude will increase from right to left. If you continued to sail west toward New Zealand, you would eventually cross the International Date Line and begin reading longitude from left to right.

Charts in use for navigation are Mercator projections, a style of projection developed by the Flemish cartographer Gerhardus Mercator (1512–94). This allows lines of latitude and longitude to appear on a perfect grid system, with the curves of longitude corrected out. The error of this is minimal on the large-scale charts in use for navigation. The error can be seen on small-scale (large-area) maps, which show Greenland to be many times larger than Australia – a result of Mercator projection distortion near the poles.

Use latitude and longitude to define any position on the globe. Latitude is recorded first; the figures for longitude second. For example, New York's rough position is 40° 30' North by 74° West. Sydney is at 34° South by 151° East.

## COMPASS VERSUS TRUE DIRECTION

Navigation begins with the compass and chart. Despite being immersed in an age of technology in which GPS and electronic charts are nearly ubiquitous, the paper chart and magnetic compass are still considered the foundation of navigation. It is from the compass that we keep track of our direction; it is on the chart that we note our position and determine our progress. (We can also use the compass to determine the direction of the wind and seas.)

To fully appreciate the compass, one needs to know its limits. How does a compass work? The earth is surrounded by a magnetic field, a flowing mass of energy that is concentrated near the North Pole. This position, which tends to wobble around over time, is called magnetic north. It is not to be confused with true north, which is the earth's actual North Pole. The card of a magnetic compass, which is immersed in mineral oil to keep it somewhat stabilized, always points to magnetic north.

So, what is the difference between magnetic and true north? Each area of the earth has different measurements for indicating the direction of magnetic north. The field of magnetic energy is not consistently flowing in the same direction other than generally northward. Charts record for us the difference between magnetic direction and true direction, which is called 'variation'. Each chart includes at least one compass rose. A compass rose includes an outer circle, which indicates true direction, and an inner circle,

## Navigational tools

Every vessel should be equipped with plotting tools for navigation. Parallel rules (A) assist in plotting a course on a chart; a calculator (B) will make time–speed–distance calculations simple; a compass (C), either hand-bearing or built into the boat, provides direction; and a pair of dividers (see page 137) can be used to measure distance on a chart.

A

B

C

which indicates magnetic direction. Within the circle is a note that describes the variation of the area of the chart. You'll notice that the arrow pointing to true north is perfectly parallel with the lines of longitude, which are printed straight up and down on the chart, whereas the arrow pointing to magnetic north is slightly skewed. The variation between magnetic and true can be as much as 15 degrees or more.

Why would the navigator care about the difference between magnetic and true direction? For one thing, direction is typically printed (in navigation books, in cruising guides, and on charts) in true, as this is a constant. Magnetic direction, on the other hand, is always on the move and is locally variable.

## Compass rose

A compass on a chart gives both magnetic (MN) and true (TN) direction.

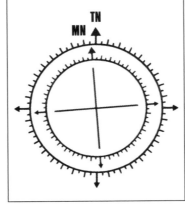

Offshore navigators, who routinely calculate celestial bearings and use books that are in true direction, typically plot courses on charts in true direction. On the other hand, coastal sailors, who more frequently use their magnetic compasses to establish fixes, typically plot in magnetic direction. Whatever you decide, it is important that you are consistent. There are compasses that are capable of factoring out magnetic error, such as the gyro-stabilized compasses used on merchant ships and electronic compasses that can be interfaced with a GPS receiver to remove the error. In this book, however, we'll concentrate on traditional navigation, assuming the navigator has a magnetic compass as standard equipment.

## The wandering pole

The earth's magnetic poles are not fixed, but move slowly with time. A scientific expedition determined that the location of the north magnetic pole in 2000 was at Lat 79° 19' N, Long 105° 26' W, on the Isachsen Peninsula of Ellef Ringnes Island in the far north of Canada. The illustration demonstrates how the magnetic pole has drifted slowly northwards throughout the twentieth century.

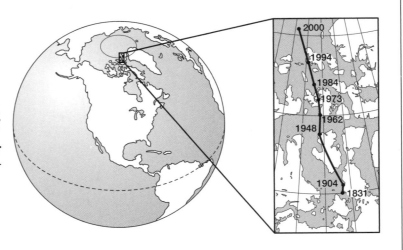

Another error that needs to be noted when converting from magnetic to true, or vice versa, is deviation. Deviation is the error that each vessel imposes on its ship's compass. Every vessel has a somewhat different deviation; engines, electronic equipment, and deck hardware can all interfere with the accuracy of a compass and result in some deviation. Each vessel with a compass installed needs to have its compass 'swung', either by a professional or by a system of checks that utilizes known direction in a given area. Once deviation is determined for all headings, a deviation table is produced. The deviation table tells the navigator how much latent error there is on given headings.

## Compass to true

First, we need to factor out the deviation on the given heading, then we factor out the variation. When converting from compass to true, we always subtract east, for both variation and deviation. Note that it is customary to refer to a magnetic direction using all three numbers, even if the first number is a zero.

Let's say we are on a course of 030° compass, and our deviation table tells us that we have 2° of easterly deviation for when we're heading northeast. Variation in the area is 10° West. By adding the easterly deviation and subtracting the westerly variation, we come up with 022° true as the course we will plot on the chart.

## True to compass

We'll use the same method, only in reverse. So, if we have westerly variation, we add it to true. (Subtract the variation if it is easterly.)

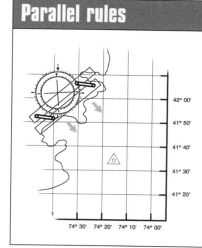

## Parallel rules

It takes some practice to effectively manage a pair of parallel rules. But they are a simple tool for plotting position, courses, and bearings to create a fix.

Then we do the same with the deviation for the particular heading the vessel is on.

Let's say we need to change course to 345° true. We need to know what course to follow on our compass. Let's assume there is 12° easterly variation and 1° of westerly deviation. By subtracting the easterly variation and adding westerly deviation, we find that we need to follow 334° on our compass.

## PLOTTING A POSITION

Now that we know the fundamentals of both positioning and direction, we can progress to plotting these figures on the chart. Most recreational sailors fall into the insidious habit of eyeballing their position on the chart, never actually taking out the plotting tools and marking a position and a course. This matters less when close to shore, but, even so, should be done only by those with practice and experience. Only when a navigator has mastered the ability to physically plot positions and courses should she deign to wing it.

The coastline you see in front of you, with its three-dimensional rocks, trees, buildings, distant hills, and underwater shoals, bears little resemblance to the two-dimensional surface of the chart, which is a stylized,

## Types of compass

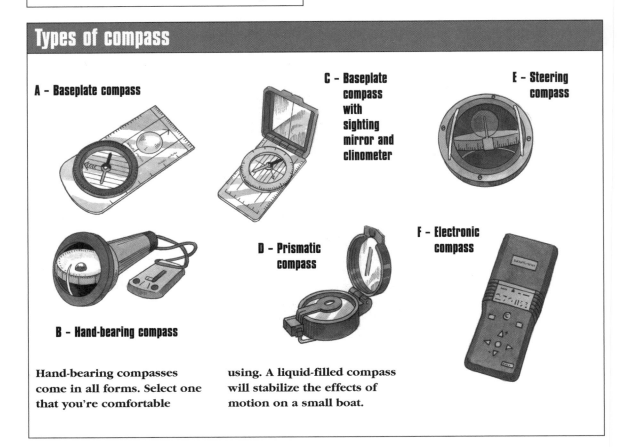

A – Baseplate compass

C – Baseplate compass with sighting mirror and clinometer

E – Steering compass

B – Hand-bearing compass

D – Prismatic compass

F – Electronic compass

Hand-bearing compasses come in all forms. Select one that you're comfortable using. A liquid-filled compass will stabilize the effects of motion on a small boat.

bird's-eye view of the coastline. It takes practice to develop an ability to translate the information on the chart to what you see in reality, and vice versa. But, if you take the time to hone plotting skills, your knowledge will serve you well in the long term.

There are two approaches to plotting a position. The first involves knowing what your coordinates are, then plotting those figures on the chart. You might do this if you have a GPS position. First read your position off the GPS receiver in latitude and longitude, then take out your plotting tools. The second method involves knowing roughly where you are, but using methods of observation to establish that position on the chart by triangulation.

Let's begin with plotting a latitude and longitude position on a chart. You can use parallel rules, navigation triangles, or whatever plotting tools are the standard in your area. In the following example, we will use parallel rules to first extend the latitude figure from the left- or right-hand side of the chart to where it will intersect the measurement of the given longitude. To do this, we first orient the parallel rules along one of the latitude lines so that they are lying exactly horizontally – east and west – on the chart. Then we 'walk' the rules up or down to our given latitude. You might need to extend the parallel rules to reach the area of the chart where the position will be. Be sure not to allow the rules to wobble, and keep them perfectly horizontal. With a sharp pencil, mark a position line along the parallel rules in the vicinity of where the longitude mark will be.

We do the same with longitude, first aligning the parallel rules perfectly north and south, and then 'walking' them to the east or west along the chart until one edge of the rules intersects our given longitude. Finally, we mark off the longitude where it intersects the latitude mark that we have already put down, carefully extending the parallel rules if the position we need to mark is not quite within reach at the rules' initial position.

## TAKING A BEARING

Now that we've plotted a position using a given latitude and longitude, as from a GPS receiver, we should work the plotting in reverse, using observation of aids to navigation – buoys and lighthouses, for example, or coastal features such as rocky points and headlands – to triangulate a position. To do this, we first need to understand how to take a magnetic bearing.

Let's assume the boat is equipped with a 'compass binnacle' – a compass mounted on its own pedestal. Stand over the binnacle so that what you are sighting is on the far side, and the binnacle is positioned between your body and the aid to navigation – a lighthouse, for example. Extend your arm and fingers in a straight line. Pointing your fingers directly towards the lighthouse, bring your hand down towards the top of the compass, and read the corresponding numbers on the compass. Your arm and hand are serving as a movable scope. The lighthouse 'bears' a given magnetic direction, say, 045° on the compass. Write this figure down on a notepad, so that it can be transferred later to the chart. Take another two bearings, selecting charted buoys or known shoals or mountaintops, then proceed to the chart. Be sure to label each bearing so that you do not confuse them with each other when you plot them on the chart. Always take at least three bearings to obtain a sound fix, and choose objects that are far apart from one another, preferably

## Measuring distance

Dividers are used to measure distance on a chart. Always use the latitude scale on the left and right sides of a chart. One minute of latitude is equal to one nautical mile. Longitude, on the other hand, is distorted as you move away from the equator.

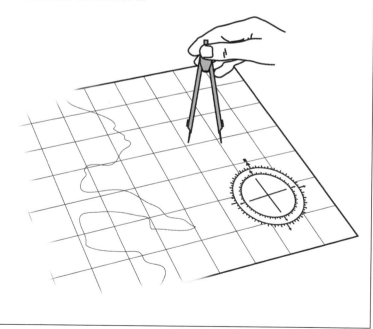

## Plotting from GPS

A GPS receiver establishes a fix using triangulation, the same principle a navigator uses for celestial fixes or by combining several magnetic bearings on a chart.

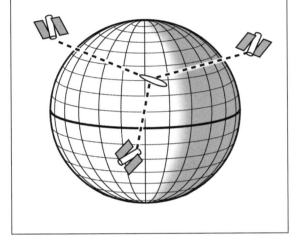

spaced evenly around the points of the compass.

To plot a bearing on the chart, first find the aid to navigation on that chart - the lighthouse, say. Next arrange your parallel rules on the magnetic compass rose so that one edge intersects the centre of the rose and the magnetic bearing (045°). Then walk the parallel rules - not allowing them to wobble from their intended angle - to the lighthouse on the chart. Once the edge of the parallels intersects the lighthouse, draw a line with a pencil onto the chart, being sure to extend it far enough into the water to your presumed position. (You should have a sense of roughly how far from the light you are, at least within a few miles.) Draw an arrow on the line that points to the light-house, indicating that that was the direction your bearing was taken. Label it with the number, in this case 045°. This is called a 'line

of position', or LOP. Your boat's position is somewhere on this line; you just don't know exactly where - yet. Repeat this process with the other bearings. Where the lines cross is your 'fix' (which is why you need at least three bearings, taken from objects that are at different points of the compass.) Label the fix with the time you took the bearings. This position is where your boat was at that time.

Bearings can also be taken using hand-bearing compasses. This is an important device to use when a compass is mounted on a bulkhead in the cockpit, making 360-degree sighting impossible. It is somewhat less accurate than a mounted binnacle - and indeed is useless on a steel-hulled boat that will make the deviation extreme - but hand-bearing compasses enable the navigator to take quick bearings and establish a fix in the same manner as described above.

### PLOTTING A COURSE

We now know where we are. Now we want to go somewhere. Let's say the boat is under way along a course of 085° true. Place the parallel rules on the compass rose so that one edge intersects the centre and passes through 085°. As we're plotting in true in this example, be sure to use the outer compass rose. Then walk the parallel rules to your fix so that one edge passes through the fix position. Extend this line with your pencil in the direction your boat is travelling - not the reciprocal, a common mistake. This line is your course line, or 'track line'. If we were plotting in magnetic direction, we would simply have used the inner compass rose. Label the track line with the course on top of the line and the speed beneath. This creates a record of your voyage directly on the chart.

### MEASURING DISTANCE

To advance your boat's position from this initial fix, you'll need to know your boat's speed. There are several ways to do this, the simplest being to consult your boat's instruments and read off the speed that appears on a display. You can also calculate your speed by timing your vessel as it advances between two objects of a known distance apart – an exact nautical mile, for example. In the old days, mariners cast over a knotted line, timing the number of knots that passed through their hands as the vessel continued on its course. The number of knots, which were spaced an even distance apart, would give them their speed. Hence the term 'knots', or nautical miles per hour.

To measure distance on a chart, you'll need a pair of dividers. If you are going to advance your course from the fix taken above and know that your speed is, say, five knots, open the dividers to five minutes of latitude, measured along the left or right side of the chart. Without moving the angle of the dividers, transfer this distance to the boat's fix, placing one end of the dividers on the fix and the other on the course line.

## GPS satellite constellation

The global positioning system consists of 24 satelllites orbiting the earth at a height of 20,200km (12,625 miles). Each satellite takes 12 hours to make a complete orbit.

## DEAD RECKONING

When you advance your course and speed, marking on the chart where you are at evenly spaced intervals (every hour on the hour, for example), this is called dead reckoning (DR). Dead reckoning is an approximate navigation, based on your course and speed. It is not based on actual fixes, beyond the original fix, and you should believe in it in the manner of the skeptic: it is sound only to the point that something better comes along. When advancing your DR position, you should plot all course changes with the times, abandoning your DR track only when you acquire another fix. A DR position is marked with a semicircle, labelled with the time.

## TIME, SPEED, AND DISTANCE

When navigating a vessel, you will frequently need to use time/space/distance equations.

If your math skills are feeble, you might consider purchasing any number of the analog devices offered in chandleries that compute these equations for you.

To solve any equation, you will need to know two out of the three values. For example, to determine how long it will take to cover a certain distance, you need to know the distance and your speed. Or, if you know distance and the time, you can figure out your speed. Or, if you know the time and speed, you can figure out the distance you will travel in this time.

To find distance (D), multiply speed (S) by time (T) in minutes, then divide by 60. Assume that your vessel is travelling 6.5 knots for 40 minutes: 6.5 x 40 = 260. Divide by 60 and you get a distance travelled of 4.3 miles.

To solve for speed (S), we multiply distance (D) by 60, then divide by the time (T). Say we know we need to travel 23 miles and want to be at this location for lunch at noon. At what rate will we need to travel if we leave the mooring at 0830? 60 x 23 = 1380. Divide this by 3.5 (it is 3$^1$/$_2$ hours until noon), which produces 394.2. This, divided by 60, is roughly 6.5 knots. If our boat makes only six knots, we might want to leave a bit earlier.

How much earlier? Divide distance (D) by speed (S) to get time (T) – roughly 3.8 hours, or 3 hours and 48 minutes.

## LOGARITHMIC SPEED SCALE

If the labours of time/speed/distance equations give you pause, consider using the logarithmic speed scale for determining the same result. Most charts have the scale printed at the bottom. A few minutes of familiarization with the scale will be a godsend for quick navigation calculations. To find time, place one point of a pair of dividers on 60 and the other on the boat's speed. Then move the dividers, without changing the angle, so that the left point falls on the distance travelled. The right point will yield the time in minutes. To solve for distance, place the right point on 60 and the left point on the boat's speed. Lift the dividers and put the right point to the allotted time; beneath the left point will be the distance in miles.

## THE SIX-MINUTE RULE

When plotting increments of time that are less than one hour, it is convenient to use six-minute increments for measuring time. That is because six minutes is one-tenth of an hour. To determine the distance run in six-minute increments, simply move the decimal place from right to left one place: For example, a boat

## Plotting a course

When you have been given a position from the GPS, use your parallel rules to plot.

(You may need to 'walk' the rules out to the area of the position.)

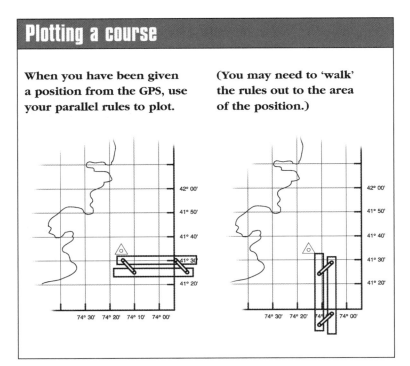

## Using landmarks

Anything that is marked on a chart – lighthouses, prominent buildings, headlands – is valuable for use in navigation. To get a 'fix', take two or three 'bearings' off such objects, and transfer the bearing lines to the chart. Where the lines cross is a 'fix'.

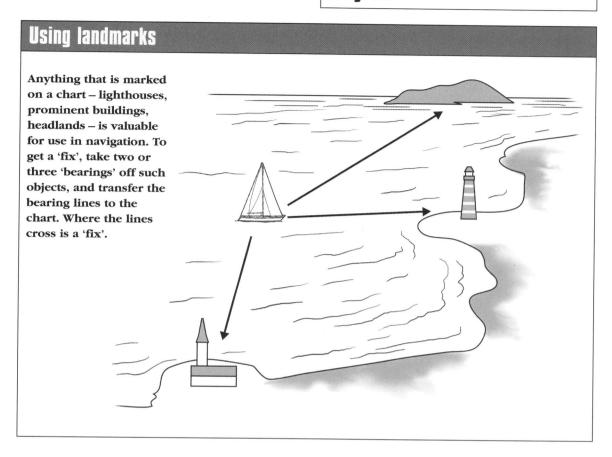

making eight knots will move .8 of a mile in six minutes; a vessel making 12 knots will make 1.2 miles in six minutes; a vessel making 22 knots will move 2.2 miles in six minutes. Using the six-minute rule allows the navigator to plan course changes in six-minute intervals: 6, 12, 18, 24, and so on.

### THE LOG

Keeping a log of a boat's progress is an essential element to good watchkeeping. While it may become tedious to log each course and sail change, it is standard to log your position regularly, perhaps every hour, making note of the weather conditions, including wind direction and velocity, and the boat's speed and position. There is

## Communication

Navigating a vessel involves frequent course changes, communicated to the helmsman by the navigator. The navigator should tell the helmsman the course by saying all three numbers: zero-five-zero, for example. The helmsman should say those numbers back in the same manner – zero-five-zero – so that the navigator is sure the course was properly understood. This may sound overzealous, but consider the consequences of being casual with the language. The same command might be expressed as 'Come to 50°', but be heard as 15° by the helmsman.

## The chart as log

A chart can serve a similar function as a logbook, albeit as an illustrated, personalized log. Long before charts were produced and updated by governments for general distribution, navigators of old maintained their charts with almost religious attention. Navigators would note prevailing wind and currents, and note land features visible from the water.

These charts were invaluable as tools and remain important historical documents. Do not be hesitant in marking up your charts, using a highlighter marker to call attention to shoals or necessary buoys.

Updating charts should be part of the routine of every navigator (recording when buoys or other navigation aids are changed); however, if you take this action one step further, you will have an opportunity to thank yourself many times over when you return to the same area at a later date. Get in the habit of interacting with your chart, circling points of interest or hazardous areas or low bridges, and the act of navigating will only increase in enjoyment and ease.

This is not to say that a chart should be scribbled on and thoughtlessly covered with flippant comments and useless trivia. Rather, a neatly detailed chart with illustrations, notes, and warnings can give pleasure upon future reflection and will serve the navigator when he returns to the same areas.

usually room to record general comments on the boat and crew's activities. It is also prudent to perform a basic boat check every hour or so, which should include a rig survey, a walk around the deck, and a tour of the belowdecks area, and notes should be made in the log. If tides are a factor in your area, note the times of high and low water on the log's daily page. Logs are also the place to record unusual incidents or emergencies.

A well-kept log can be used to reconstruct a vessel's position at a given time, allowing the navigator to refresh his knowledge of an area when he returns at another time. Good anchorages, notes on whether facilities are available at a certain location, or discussion of the weather and its effect on the boat contribute to the boat's living history. If you're heading out for a few days' sail, a log that carefully noted positions will assist you on your return trip.

### ESTIMATED POSITION

An estimated position is not guesswork; it involves combining a single bearing of a fixed object, such as a buoy or other navigational aid, with the DR track. An estimated position is one step up from a dead reckoning in terms of dependency. It allows the navigator to gain a better sense of where he is when only one line of position is available.

Plot the bearing in the usual way. Where it intersects the DR track is where the estimated position is. An estimated position is marked with a square and labelled with the time.

### LEEWAY

Leeway is the amount that a vessel slips sideways as a result of wind and waves. Leeway needs to be compensated for, either by estimation or by taking a series of fixes to establish the exact angle – which could be anywhere from 2°-3° for a performance race boat in calm conditions to as much as 20°-30° for an older design not built for going to windward.

## OPERATOR ERROR

No one is perfect, let alone a person who is attempting to steer a large object under sail power in fickle conditions, perhaps at night, in waves that attempt to throw her from her perch. Operator error is a very real error that every navigator should consider when laying out the DR line. When preparing to plot the DR position, the navigator should ask the helmsman what his course steered was. Course steered is based on the course ordered, but is the average that the helmsman was able to keep. He should have a sense of whether he was wandering from the ordered course in one direction or the other. The helmsman might admit that, despite a course ordered of 050°, he was actually able to steer only 055°, for example. The navigator should plot this course – the course actually steered – as the DR course.

## CURRENT

Current is the invisible foe. Generated by tide or river flow, currents will carry any vessel in the direction it is flowing. Where wind direction is measured in the direction it is coming from, current is measured in the direction it is flowing to. (A northeast wind and a southwest current are travelling in the same direction.) The presence of a current

## Using a sounding lead

Captain James Cook, and numerous other explorers both before and after him, used a sounding lead for approaching unfamiliar coastlines. When Cook ventured from England in 1768 aboard *Endeavour*, one-third of the world's shores were unknown to Europeans. The continents of Australia and Antarctica, and most of the islands of the North and South Pacific, including all of New Zealand, had never been mapped. Cook proceeded cautiously, using a sounding lead to feel his way along the shores and recording the depth. His charts remained in use until the mid-1990s, as detailed in Tony Horwitz's popular book *Blue Latitudes*.

A sounding lead is a lead weight attached to the end of a lightweight line. The lead is hollow on the bottom, allowing it to be plugged with a sticky substance such as tallow, butter, or bacon grease. The line is marked with strips of cloth or paint every fathom (6ft). Toss the weight off the bow, taking note of the depth each time the lead lands on the bottom. Examination of the grease on the bottom will tell you what the bottom is like in this area. Consult your chart: it should tell you what type of bottom to expect.

can often be observed on the surface. A wind opposing the flow of the current will typically stack up short, choppy waves. A strong current will drag over buoys or flow visibly around fixed beacons, creating a V-shaped swirl in the water.

There are ways to calculate the effects of current. Current is defined by its 'set' and 'drift'. The set is the direction it is flowing; the drift is the rate it is flowing. Most governments publish tidal current tables for their surrounding waters, allowing the navigator to determine in advance the set and drift of the current in specific geographic areas. Guide books can also be useful for this purpose. Bear in mind that currents are listed in true direction.

If you don't have access to these books, or if you want to check on the set and drift of a current as it exists in reality, you can determine the set and drift by setting up a vector diagram. After sailing through an area where current is present, check your position, either by taking bearings or using an electronic device. If you are appreciably off where your DR position tells you should be, and leeway and operator error cannot account for this, you have been set by the current.

What course should you steer to make good the course you want? You need to factor the current's set and drift out of your course and speed to establish a sound course made good. First, it is helpful to visualize the effects of the current. A current that is setting in the same direction as your boat will increase your speed over the bottom; if it is setting in the opposite direction, it will decrease your speed. If it is setting from the beam, it will push your vessel sideways, but if it is setting at a 45-degree angle off either bows, it will both slow the vessel and affect its course.

### Plotting set and drift

To plot a set and drift diagram, first measure off the desired course made good, say 120°, drawing the line as long as you expect to travel in one hour, say, 6

## Set and drift

When it is necessary to compensate for the effects of current, you need to factor out the current's 'set' – its direction – and its 'drift' – or velocity.

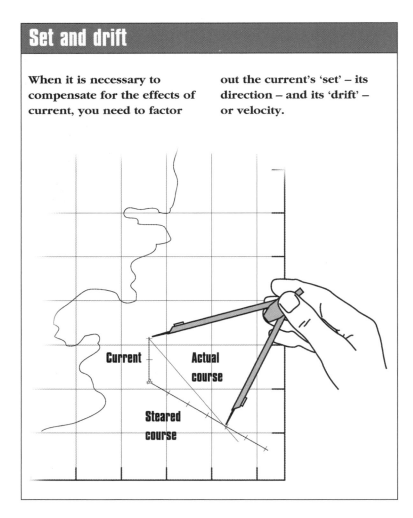

Current

Actual course

Steared course

# Anchor watch bearings

If you choose to anchor your vessel for any period of time, it will be imperative to be certain that the boat is secure. As discussed in other parts of this chapter, check the anchor rode – by placing your hand on it – to feel for possible dragging.

Maintain a visual lookout at least once per hour – or more frequently if conditions warrant – taking note not only of your own boat's position, but also that of other vessels in the area. If you see a boat dragging, the operator may not realize. Attempt to get the attention of the crew using VHF Channel 16 or Channel 09, or by shouting – whatever it takes to get them to help themselves from dragging into other boats or ashore.

One way to ensure that your vessel is holding position is to set up a series of bearings for the crew to monitor. If you are anchored for the night, it will be important to note the bearings by their light characteristics, as darkness will likely prevent clear sight of unlit objects. If anchoring during the day, bearings can include tall buildings or spires, prominent points of land, buoys, or even treetops. (Whatever you choose, be sure that the crew knows which bearings are which; it might be necessary to describe the object in writing.)

Take at least three bearings. Choose objects that are evenly spaced apart so that the compass is divided roughly in thirds. This will give the best fix, as no two bearings will be reciprocal to each other.

Write the bearings down in the log with instructions about how frequently you would like the bearings to be taken, every hour, for example. Leave a space in the log next to each entry for crew members' initials. Leave instructions for the crew members to wake the captain in the event that bearings have appreciably changed.

Be sure that each crew member knows how to take an accurate bearing. Show them how to sight across the compass, using an extended arm as a guide, and reading off a number from the compass card. If the boat is not equipped with a compass binnacle, which allows you to walk completely around the compass, a hand-bearing compass will be necessary.

A change in the bearings may not necessarily mean that the boat is dragging anchor. If the wind has shifted – or dropped – the boat will likely swing around on its anchor. This will change the anchor bearings. Take care that the vessel's new position does not bring it dangerously close to submerged ledges, shallow water, or other vessels.

miles if you are making 6 knots. Plot this line on the chart from your fix position. Your observation has shown that the current is setting 000° at a rate of two knots.

Plot this line, drawn exactly 2 miles long, extending from your fix position as well. You should now have two lines from the fix: one that extends 6 miles in a direction of 120° (the course you want to make good) and one that extends 000° (north) for two miles (the current's set and drift).

Set your dividers at 6 miles (your boat's speed through the water, as calculated by your log), placing one end at the northward end of the set and drift line and making a mark with the other end where it intersects the 120° course line (if the dividers don't intersect the 120° course line, simply extend that line a bit).

Now place your parallel rules between the end of the set and drift line and this new mark, and walk them through the centre of

# Radar

In the age of GPS, is radar still considered a viable tool? The answer is an emphatic yes. Where GPS will tell you where satellites think you are, often within just a few feet of pinpoint accuracy, only radar will tell you exactly where you are in relation to other objects: rocky shores and other vessels.

Radar units are a bit more expensive than GPS devices, ranging between about $700 and up to $3000 or much more, depending on the bells and whistles. Yet they are well worth the expense if you take the time to learn how to use some of their basic functions.

A radar antenna sends and receives microwave energy pulses at the speed of light, 964 feet per microsecond (one millionth of a second). For each degree of rotation, the antenna sends and receives approximately 30 snapshots of the area, producing a 'picture' on the scope, or screen. By timing the pulses, which are at a constant speed, and keeping track of the angles, radar does two basic things: it measures the relative angle of objects from the boat's heading, and it measures its distance away. These are called 'bearing' and

'range', respectively. To measure the bearing of an object, the EBL (electronic bearing line) function is used. Your radar set will most likely be 'head up' – as opposed to 'north up' – which means that the line that extends from the centre of the screen to the top always points in the same direction as your boat. When you align the EBL on another object and measure its relative bearing, you need to add your boat's heading to this number to determine the object's magnetic bearing. This number can then be plotted on the chart and used like any other bearing.

To establish an object's range, or distance away, spin the VRM (variable range marker) dial out to the object, and read off the distance. You can do this for any number of objects. Note the object and its range, and plot it on the chart. Using a pair of dividers, measure off the range on the chart's scale, then place one tip of the dividers on the buoy or point of land, or whatever it was you saw on the radar screen. Now strike an arc with the other tip of the dividers. By combining this range arc with an electronic bearing – or with a visual bearing – you can establish a fix. Mark it with the time.

Radar is a versatile tool. It can be used for collision avoidance, by keeping track of another vessel's relative position, and can also be interfaced with other electronics such as GPS and electronic charts. There are whole books and courses offered on the use of radar. If you invest in a radar set, take the time to learn its functions and limitations.

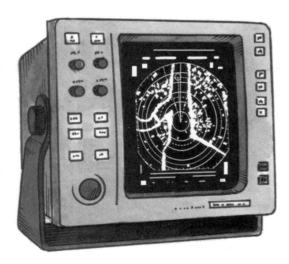

the compass rose. Read where the edge of the rules intersects the compass rose. This is the course to steer.

Measuring the distance along the 120° line from your fix position to the intersection mark will yield your speed made good (the speed you will actually make over the ground, given the combination of your boat's course and speed through the water and the current's set and drift).

## DANGER BEARINGS AND DANGER CIRCLES

Bearings can be used for other purposes besides establishing a fix. If you want to avoid a hazard, shoal, or rocky point, passing it by at a certain distance, take bearings to establish a safety zone around these objects. You can set up a bearing in advance, running it out on the chart and checking on the object's bearing as you move within range. When the object bears the angle you set up, it is safe to turn.

## USING SOUNDINGS

If your vessel is equipped with a depth sounder or echo sounder or if you have a sounding lead aboard, you can use soundings to monitor your vessel's progress. As a chart gives depths, you can use this information to intersect a bearing line, thereby giving a reasonable fix. If you are approaching a coastline from offshore, set up a bearing on a fixed object ashore at the same time that you monitor your depth.

Let's say you're approaching a lighthouse that marks the entrance to a harbour. You extend your DR track to where you want to enter the harbour. Notice the point at which it will cross a given depth, also called a fathom curve, say 10 fathoms (or 60 feet). Now, as your vessel approaches, monitor the depth until you have sounded 10 fathoms. Immediately get a bearing on the lighthouse, and plot the line. Where the bearing line crosses the 10-fathom curve is where your fix is. Label it with the time.

# CHAPTER 9

# Surviving at sea

**A survival situation is defined as a scenario in which all one's energy is focused on a fight for life. Such scenarios might include capsize, collision, grounding, falling overboard, or even a simple infection that is not cared for and allowed to progress to life-threatening stages. Common sense is the best defence against such peril, and, despite the risks, a well-prepared sailor can expect to enjoy a lifetime of safe boating activity.**

This chapter describes some of the more common boating accidents and how to respond to them in a way that will save your boat from being lost or destroyed. The decision to abandon ship in favour of a tiny inflatable raft or other small craft should be seen as a last resort. Although this chapter will also explain how to survive certain open-water emergencies, its primary purpose is to help you avoid – at all costs – scenarios that require those survival skills.

In the developed world, we have come to rely on a large safety net – the international rescue services that can pluck hapless sailors

## Teamwork

To avoid situations such as man overboard or other injuries, it is imperative that the crew communicates effectively, especially in periods of heavy weather or during sail manoeuvres such as tacking and anchoring.

from the sea many thousands of miles from land. We often read in our newspapers about these rescues, which may involve multinational efforts, often including navy and coastguard ships, fixed-wing aircraft, and a team of helicopters, to recover sailors who have been dismasted in the middle of the Southern Ocean or capsized in the tumultuous waters of the North Atlantic. In many respects, these reports serve to lull the public into a false sense of security, encouraging them to believe that professional rescue is just a phone call away.

This is sometimes true, particularly in coastal waters, but each person who decides to be a sailor, to cast off from the mooring and turn his bow away from the shore, must think of himself as autonomous, solely responsible for his own safety and for the safety of his vessel and crew.

## Coast guard to the rescue

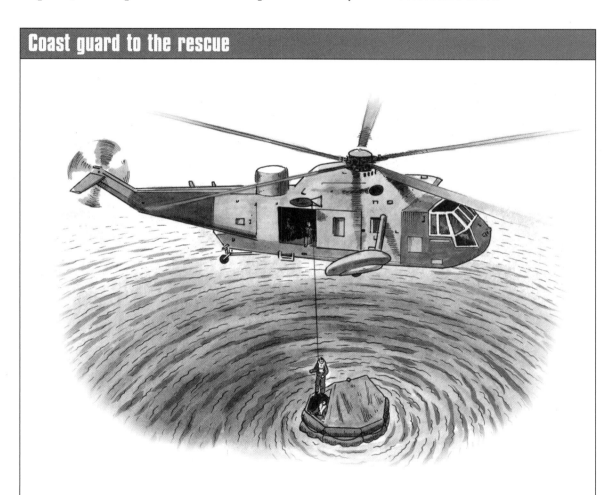

Being airlifted from your boat or a raft is a last-resort strategy employed by the coast guard. If you are in such a situation, the coast guard rescue teams will communicate exactly how they would like you to behave so that they are able to help you efficiently and safely.

What knowledge and equipment do you need to be independent? These pages will make every effort to answer the question, but the variability of the wind and waves, and the numerous types of vessels make this a substantial – perhaps impossible – task. In the end, it is up to the individual to decide if he, his crew, and his vessel are ready for the marine environment.

## GROUNDING

Even the most well-prepared and cautious sailors go aground at some point in their sailing careers. Sooner or later, if you spend enough time on the water, your keel will touch bottom. Once you're comfortable with this fact – that grounding a boat does not mean you should abandon the sea forever – the terror of grounding will be somewhat ameliorated.

This isn't to say that grounding is not hazardous; it is, and every skipper should do whatever it takes to avoid grounding her vessel. But most boats are built well, built to withstand being tossed around by the sea, even when the keel drives into a rocky ledge. If you do go aground, it is essential that you remain calm, consider the situation in a way that prioritizes what needs to be done, then act decisively.

The first principle to understand is the difference between static and dynamic forces on your boat. If you sail a keelboat, you know that, when the boat comes out of the water, it can be stowed on stands, the keel supporting the weight of the boat without causing damage. The same is true of a beach or ledge: your boat can be grounded, supported on an even keel by the buoyancy of the hull, and not be damaged. Boats are damaged when they strike the bottom with force, whether as a result of boat speed or the pounding of waves.

If you strike a rock at five knots, remain stuck fast, and are then pounded by a series of swells or other waves that lift the boat and drop it, serious damage can result.

## Seeking assistance

If your boat grounds in such a situation, anyone who is standing will probably be thrown off her feet. People sitting in the cockpit will be tossed forward, especially if they are not holding on to anything. If the bottom is rocky, the motion can be quite violent. If the boat's keel grounds in sand or mud, the motion will be far less sudden, so

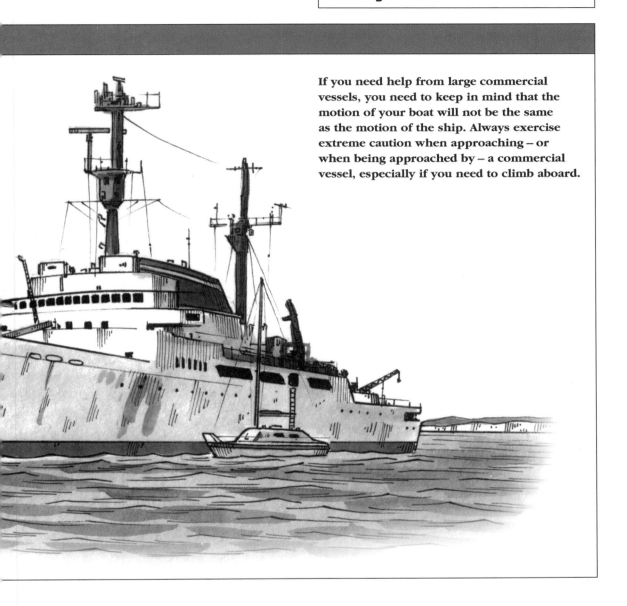

If you need help from large commercial
vessels, you need to keep in mind that the
motion of your boat will not be the same
as the motion of the ship. Always exercise
extreme caution when approaching – or
when being approached by – a commercial
vessel, especially if you need to climb aboard.

subtle, even, that it may take a moment for
crew to realize that the boat is actually
aground; you might think instead that you've
been caught on fishing gear.

Once you have realized that you are
aground, there will be ways to free your
vessel. First, consider the direction of the
wind. How can you trim your sails that will
most effectively push your boat back into
deeper water? You might have to back the jib
or release the main.

If you have an engine, start it immediately.
Before engaging the engine, be sure that the
propeller is not in danger of striking rocks or
fouling in kelp. Next, consider the direction
you want to move the boat – ahead or astern –

before actually engaging the gear. If you have grounded in mud, you will want to be sure that your propeller's wash will not further bury the keel. Whenever you engage the engine to recover buoyancy following a grounding, always increase rpm in small increments. You want to come off slowly and not stress your engine and propulsion system – the transmission, shaft pin/key, and propeller – to the point that you add to your problems.

If manoeuvring with your sails and working your engine (at the same time, if necessary)

has not worked, you should consider setting an anchor. If you are towing a dinghy, it might make sense to have someone row the anchor away from the boat in a direction that you want the boat to come off.

You also want to be aware of the tide level. If you have grounded during a rising tide, you want to ensure that your boat is not pushed further aground. You want to stabilize the position so that the rise of the tide will lift the boat clear. If the tide is falling – and, given Murphy's Law, it probably is – your

## Plugging a hole

If you need to perform damage control methods on your boat, you'll need to be creative to stem the flow of water. Each through-hull fitting should have its own dedicated wooden plug. Tie a plug of the appropriate size to each such valve.

situation is somewhat more urgent. Each minute that you remain aground means slightly less water under your keel. If your vessel is indeed hard aground on a falling tide, your best efforts might be expended by ensuring that the vessel is not too damaged by the exposed bottom upon which the hull will come to rest.

At all times, you should keep the safety of your crew foremost in your mind. If the vessel remains stuck fast, you should not hesitate to reach for the radio and call for help. Have everyone put on life jackets. Your first assistance is likely to come from other vessels in the area, the operators of which can provide a tow, take passengers off, or assist in setting more anchors. Do not let your wounded pride prevent you from asking for help. Remember, everyone touches bottom at some point. Once it happens, your response to the situation is far more important than preserving your pride.

If you have grounded and the boat slides free – either thanks to your manoeuvres on the sails or because of external causes – you should first check with each crew member to see that no one has sustained serious injury. Next consider the boat's safety, and check for leaks. When a boat grounds, excessive dynamic energy can loosen seams, fastenings, and joints, letting water come into the hull. Open the floorboards in the cockpit, and look for water. Find the lowest part of the bilge, usually about one-third of the way forward from the stern, and see if the water level in the bilge is rising. If your boat has a cabin, go below immediately and again look for water.

If you see that the water level is rising, ensure that your pumps are engaged. If you have electric pumps mounted in the bilge, see that they are operating effectively. If you have back-up pumps, either electric or hand-powered, set them up as well.

At all times, keep your crew informed. Keep in mind that you don't need to do everything yourself; give your crew tasks, such as pumping or monitoring the water level or communicating on the radio if the flooding is out of control.

You should make every effort to find the source of the leak. If a through-hull fitting has been damaged, check whether it can be plugged with a wooden plug or other object. If you see an open seam, set up a bracing system or try to patch the leak with underwater epoxy. Keep in mind that you want your bilge water to remain more or

## Avoiding grounding

Grounding a boat is usually the result of a variety of factors that conspire against the skipper at the wrong time. With experience, the seasoned sailor can begin to sense when a situation is slipping towards confusion and chaos. If you have a hunch that your boat is not exactly in the position you thought it was – and there is shallow water in the vicinity – stop your boat and determine your position. This creeping suspicion that all is not right with your navigation may be exacerbated by other circumstances, such as strong wind or numerous other vessels in the area.

If you're distracted – watching other vessels, putting a reef in the mainsail, or attending to a seasick passenger – your full attention has been diverted from your navigation. Being aware of all these different elements when sailing a boat is called, in the parlance of professional marine investigators and regulators, situational awareness. When there's a lot going on, it will take extra energy on the part of the skipper to remain focused and aware of her resources. When in doubt about your boat's position, stop the boat and get your bearings. The slight delay will be far better than the delay – and damage – caused by grounding.

## Fire

Fire aboard a boat is an extreme hazard. A blanket (obviously not one made of flammable material) can effectively smother a small grease fire and will not necessitate the use of messy chemical extinguishers.

less clean, however, so that your pumps can continue to operate without being clogged.

If a flooding situation has deteriorated to a point that your best efforts cannot keep up with the flow of water, it is time to re-evaluate your options. Grounding your boat on a beach – preferably one that is protected from the direct impact of swells and large waves – might save your boat from sinking. Or other vessels, including coast guard rescue vessels, can deliver high-powered pumps.

Again, consider all your resources before giving up hope. If the vessel is indeed sinking out from under you, you'll want to

## Roadside assistance for sailors

Several maritime organizations, some for profit and some not, offer towing and salvage services to their memberships. In exchange for a yearly fee, these organizations will respond to your VHF or cell phone call and deploy their high-powered rescue vessels to assist you.

They can supply spare fuel when your tanks have run dry and the wind has died, deliver powerful pumps for a flooding emergency, or tow you back to shore.

announce your situation – Mayday – over the radio and prepare to abandon ship. Grab your abandon ship bag; be sure that all crew's life jackets are properly secured, and continue to think about solutions. Your vessel may have enough reserve buoyancy to remain afloat. Do not abandon the vessel for a life raft or dinghy until you are certain that the boat will go down.

## FIRE

Any fire aboard a small vessel is a serious emergency. A vessel is built of combustible material – wood or fibreglass composite – and there are any number of combustibles to be found below decks, including oil, diesel fuel, gasoline, propane, and assorted equipment and clothing.

One way to minimize the impact of fire is to run a vessel downwind. This will lessen the effects of the fire being fanned. In the early twentieth century, a fire on the steamship *General Slocum* in New York harbour killed hundreds of passengers, many of them children, because the vessel was kept steaming straight into the wind, which spread the fire throughout the vessel, engulfing it in flames. Had the ship been turned downwind immediately, the vessel would barely have felt the effects of the wind, and the fire could probably have been contained.

Fire needs three elements to burn: heat, fuel, and oxygen. Remove just one of these, and the fire will be extinguished.

Fires can start for any number of reasons, but they are especially common in engine

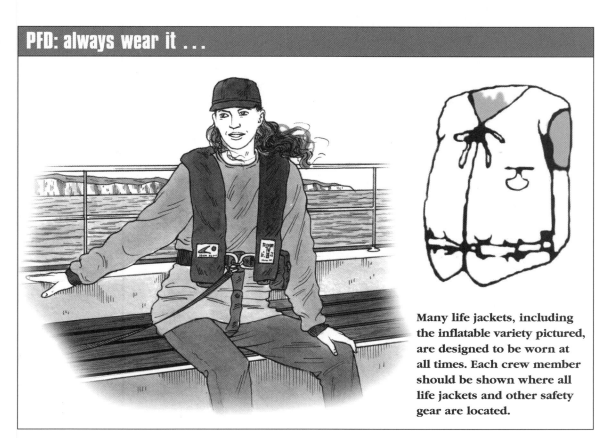

**PFD: always wear it . . .**

Many life jackets, including the inflatable variety pictured, are designed to be worn at all times. Each crew member should be shown where all life jackets and other safety gear are located.

## The jury rig

Accidents happen, and you need to respond in an effective manner. If your vessel is dismasted, for example, you may still be able to effect a jury rig by bracing up a stub of a mast and rigging your sails to that.

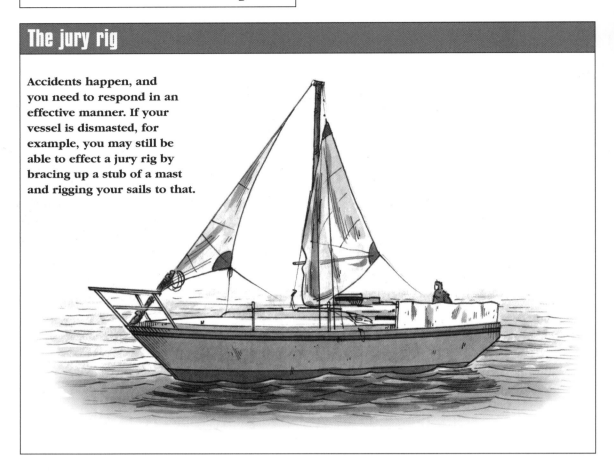

spaces and galleys. If you have a fire in the engine room, shut down the engine and shut off the supply. Direct a portable fire extinguisher at the base of the blaze. If firefighting efforts are not working, attempt to cut off the air supply by sealing the engine space. If your vessel is equipped with a gasoline engine, shut off the blower that is supplying fresh air.

During each drill, be sure that your fire extinguishers have not passed their expiration dates. If equipped with a gauge, be sure that the level is within normal limits.

Galley fires can often be extinguished by smothering the blaze with bicarbonate of soda (baking soda), sand, or a blanket. Don't hesitate to throw the burning object overboard, whatever it is.

Water is effective as an extinguishing agent against so-called Class A fires – burning wood, paper, or other natural substances. Do not throw water at an electrical or petroleum-based fire. Remember, too, that a burning frying pan or a pool of oil in the bilge can be flared up by a stream of water, spreading the fire. That being said, water can be used to cool the surroundings of a petroleum fire.

Burning petroleum products – Class B fires – should be extinguished by carbon dioxide ($CO_2$), foam or dry chemical. $CO_2$ is an effective extinguisher because it displaces oxygen. If it is used in an open fire, however, flare-up can occur if the fire is not completely extinguished because the $CO_2$ does not serve to cool the combustible material. Foam is an effective agent against petroleum fires. It sits atop the blaze and smothers the fire. Be aware that dry chemicals can damage an engine, electronics, and other systems.

Foam should not be used on electrical – Class C – fires because it can conduct electricity. Large electrical fires are less common on boats because of low voltage; however, electrical sparks can set off other classes of fires.

Vessels up to 8m (26ft) in length should be equipped with at least two portable fire extinguishers, according to the American Boat and Yacht Council.

## EMERGENCY DRILLS

The importance of practising for emergencies cannot be overstated. Groundings, fires, man overboard (MOB), and collisions are all events that will be rife with confusion. The response to most emergencies cannot be completely scripted in advance, but, if you and your crew have been training to respond to emergencies, you will be several steps ahead in the process of damage control. You should practise emergency drills often, at the beginning of each boating season and then periodically throughout the season.

For MOB recovery drills, throw a flotation cushion over the side and manoeuvre the vessel back to its position. Practise throwing the life ring. Practise rigging the MOB recovery gear, whether you have a life sling–style apparatus or a boarding ladder. After recovering the dummy, have a discussion about how it went. See if anyone has thoughts about how the drill could have gone smoother.

When you have fire drills, be sure that each fire extinguisher is located and that all buckets are set up for possible use.

Remember that a fire aboard a boat might lead to a flooding emergency, either because hoses can burn through and allow water to enter the hull or because you might be throwing buckets of water into the boat.

When you have drills to respond to a flooding emergency, don't just locate your reserve pumps; set them up for actual pumping. Check the location of each through-hull. Consider where to ground your vessel if the flooding becomes extreme. One way to ground a vessel with minimal damage is to navigate alongside a seawall of heavy dock. To do this, approach the dock as though preparing to come alongside, fenders deployed and dock lines at the ready. Instead of tying alongside, allow it to come alongside and continue moving towards shore. Once the vessel has grounded, secure the lines to the dock. Be sure to have enough lines, at appropriate angles and to secure attachment points, to ensure that the vessel will not fall away from the dock.

Vessels that are equipped with a fin keel and spade rudder can be seriously damaged by purposeful grounding. Do this only as a last resort if pumps are not available.

### Launching a life raft

A inflatable life raft will need to be tied to the boat prior to being deployed. Otherwise, it can blow away in strong winds. Life rafts are equipped with a knife for cutting loose once everyone is aboard.

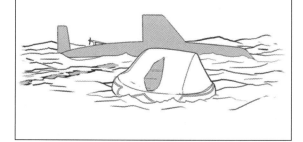

## DISMASTING

When your vessel's mast has become damaged to the point that it is no longer capable of carrying sail, you will need to consider jury rigging. A dismasting incident can be the result of any number of factors, including excessive rolling or pitching, where the snapping motion of the waves deliver excessive loads on your rig; capsize; and strong winds such as in squalls, gales, or thunderstorms.

Because your rig is held in place by a series of metal wires, the rig will probably stay attached to the boat, albeit hanging in a precarious position. This tangle of wire and splintered wood or aluminium can be an extreme hazard.

Your tool kit should include bolt cutters or a hacksaw powerful enough to cut through the wire rigging. If you can salvage your mast by cutting away the rig and lashing it to the deck, it may serve a future use. You will be able to salvage the fittings for the replacement mast, and, if you still need your sails to get back to shore, you may need the mast pieces to effect a jury rig.

There are countless tales of dismasted sailboats limping to shore after thousands of miles of jury-rigged sailing. Even if you are only on a day's sail a mile or two from land, you should still attempt to stabilize your rig. If you don't, the jagged mast can puncture the hull and add a flooding emergency to your already substantial troubles.

Your new rig will not be as efficient as your original one; however, you may be able to sail your vessel on at least a beam reach if you can get some sail area up on a makeshift mast. You may have to exchange sails, using an inverted or sideways jib lashed to the shortened mast. If your vessel is dismasted, contact rescue services, even if you are not in imminent danger. They can prepare rescue vessels in case the situation worsens or offer feedback on where and how to direct your vessel to the nearest port.

## COLLISION

If you collide with another vessel, your first concern for the boat - after every crew member is confirmed safe - is with a flooding emergency. The most vulnerable part of your vessel is the side of the hull below the waterline, where there is little structural bracing to absorb the direct shock of collision, particularly if it is delivered by the pointed end of another vessel. Large, gaping holes can sink a small vessel in minutes, but there may be a few damage control tasks that are worth considering. If your vessel has sustained a hole on the starboard side, will the hole be above the level of the water if you continue sailing - back to harbour - on a starboard tack?

One way to induce a boat's heel in such a situation is to have crew members sit on the low side of the boat. Also, consider packing heavy equipment, such as an anchor and water bottles, on the port side.

You can also use a sail or tarp to wrap the hull in such a way as to prevent most of the water from coming in the hole. The pressure of the water outside the hole will help to keep the fabric snug against the hole. The fabric will also need to be tied down - under the hull as well as over the deck, with lines that run fore and aft.

If your vessel has become tangled with another, concentrate your efforts on freeing your vessel, using hacksaws or other tools to bring them apart. While locked together, your vessels will lack the ability to navigate and could be swept aground. Always contact authorities following a collision - and make sure that you log the name of the other vessel and her crew. If there is time, be sure to log contact information of the skipper for further communication once damage control efforts have been stabilized.

If collision is imminent, do not attempt to use your arms and legs to soften the blow. Limbs will be crushed between the vessels. Any damage to the boat is far less in value -

# Using a life sling

You will not be able to lift a person bodily out of the water. If the victim is unable to climb aboard himself, it may be necessary to winch the person aboard using a halyard winch attached to a life-sling device.

both monetarily and otherwise – than the potential injuries to you. Let the boats collide. You might try, if there's time, to turn into the collision so that the bow of your vessel takes the worst of the hit. Not only does a bow present a smaller target, but also the bow of a vessel has more reinforcement than the sides of the hull.

Be sure that crew members are off the foredeck and hanging on to the boat tightly. Just as in a grounding situation, the force of a collision can be extremely violent. A head-on collision will have the force of the combined speeds of each boat.

## RECOVERING A CREW OVERBOARD

An MOB emergency is life-threatening. Even if the person is a strong swimmer and goes over the side on a summer's day, there are numerous factors that make recovery difficult. Among these factors are cold water; waves the height of which will limit visibility of the person's head in the water; strong winds; inexperienced crew; injuries sustained by the person as he went into the water; the fitness of the person (whether he's a strong swimmer and in good physical condition); and the preparedness of the boat and crew to deal with such an emergency.

## Capsized

Always remain with your vessel even if it is capsized. Try to right the vessel yourself, and signal for help with any means available.

- When a person goes over the side, announce 'Man overboard!' with urgency so that each member of the crew, whether on deck or below, understands the nature of the emergency.
- Throw a life ring over the side, directly at the person or in his general direction. Keep the end of the life ring's tag line on the boat. If the victim is able to grab the life ring, stop the boat immediately, as you don't want to drag him through the water.
- Designate one person as the pointer, whose sole job it is to point at the person's head or where his head was last seen if it is lost between the waves.
- Stop the boat. If you have an engine, start it and drop the sails. If you need the sails for manoeuvring, sheet them in tight, and manoeuvre back to the person in the water. This can be accomplished any number of ways, including sailing in tight circles around the person until the vessel is close enough or performing a figure-of-eight turn, in which the vessel comes about, crossed back over its course, then rounds up into the wind abeam of the MOB.
- After throwing the life ring, throw a few other buoyant objects overboard as well – seat cushions, life jackets, and so on. This will give the person more objects to grab if needed and also give the crew a bit of a trail back to the area where the person went over.
- When recovering a person in the water, do so with the vessel 'in irons', its sails no longer full because the boat is pointed directly into the wind, or with the person on the lee, or downwind, side. (If you manoeuvre the boat so that the person is upwind of the stopped vessel, the vessel will probably drift away from the person faster than he can swim – if, indeed, he is still able to swim.)
- Prepare the life sling or other recovery equipment, including the vessel's board-ing ladder. The victim will be scared and exhausted, and will be unable to bring himself back aboard.
- Once aboard, treat the victim for hypothermia (see below), getting him out of wet clothes and into dry ones, and give him something warm to drink. Proceed to shore for possible medical attention – or a chance for the person to stand on dry land and recover his composure.

## CAPSIZE

If your vessel is knocked down by strong winds, or overwhelmed by the waves so that it 'turns turtle', you should remain with the boat. If you and the crew are not already wearing life jackets, it is imperative that they are put on immediately and adjusted so that all straps are snug. Always secure the leg straps on a child's life jacket; otherwise, the child can easily slip through and drown.

First, send off a Mayday call by VHF radio. Remain with the vessel. If you start to swim towards land, even land that appears close, you risk becoming separated from each other; you risk becoming exhausted; and you risk suffering from hypothermia, even if the water is relatively warm.

All of these risks will present unnecessary challenges to your rescuers. If you are clinging to the overturned hull of a vessel that appears to be remaining afloat, try to climb out of the water so that you minimize your exposure to the cold water.

Some overturned vessels can be righted. If your vessel has a keel, it will want to come back up. It may need a little help, especially if the sails are full of water. Do not position yourself under the keel. The vessel could snap upright quickly.

If the vessel has a daggerboard, try righting the vessel by standing on the overturned hull, gripping the daggerboard and leaning backwards. Shifting your weight to one side could be all the help the boat

## Abandoning ship

If you find that it is necessary to abandon ship, deploy your life raft after tying the painter to the boat. Grab your abandon ship bag, and board the raft.

It may not be necessary – or even advisable – to disconnect yourself from your boat. Do so only when absolutely necessary, like if the boat is in danger of sinking.

needs to regain its stability. Once the vessel is righted, the cockpit will be full of water, which will need to be baled out. The act of baling, and any other vigorous activity such as jury-rigging the damaged rig, can help a frightened or demoralized crew member to not feel helpless.

### Survival in the water

If your boat sinks and you are adrift in the waves with your crew, make every effort to stay together. Gather together in a tight circle, gripping each other's life jackets. If there is line or strapping available, tie each person's life jacket to another person's, so that, if a person's grip fails, he or she will not easily drift away.

The circle should be extremely tight so that body warmth is conserved. If you're alone in the water, hug your life jacket and curl yourself into a ball, tucking legs and arms tightly to your chest. This limits the surface area exposed to the water and insulates your blood in your torso.

winds and is likely to be capsized or rolled off wave crests.

But if you do find yourself in a raft, your focus should be to keep yourself warm and nourished, and to communicate your position to the rescuers, via whatever means available – VHF radio, cell phone, flares, signal mirror, or water dye. If you are sailing in the tropics, warmth is less of an issue; exposure to the sun is the big danger. It is possible to survive many days, weeks, even months in a life raft if you have a few tools such as fishhooks, some fishing line, and, most important, a will to live. Just ask American sailor Steve Callahan, who survived 76 days adrift in the Atlantic Ocean after his sailboat sank, capturing fish and birds for nourishment. Callahan later wrote a book about his experience called, appropriately, *Adrift*.

## HYPOTHERMIA

Hypothermia is a life-threatening condition, in which the body's core temperature is lowered. It is caused by prolonged exposure to the elements, such as cold wind or water. Hypothermia is especially hazardous to sailors. First, it attacks the ability to stay alert, meaning that you lose the ability to make sound decisions. Secondly, it limits a person's small motor skills, so tying lines becomes difficult. What's more, the ability to navigate or handle sail can be impaired, so a person who is hypothermic is a liability both to herself and to the safety of the vessel itself. A person who has been exposed to a cold wind for a long period of time, perhaps several hours, is in danger of becoming hypothermic. Add rain or flying spray and you introduce another level or risk.

The body's first response to exposure is shivering – moving the muscles vigorously to generate heat. If a person's body has cooled to 32°–35°C (90°–95°F), she will be shivering. Her skin will be cool to the touch, and speech will probably be slurred. Once a person's core temperature drops below 32°C (90°F),

## Survival in a life raft

As stated numerous times in this book, you should leave your vessel in favour of a raft only as the last possible resort. In *The Annapolis Book of Seamanship*, John Rousmaniere explains that, during the storm that overtook the 1979 Fastnet race, several sailors who had abandoned their vessels for life rafts later died – but their vessels survived the storm.

A life raft is small and unstable. In strong winds, it will be lashed by the full fury of the

## The HELP position

This position works in two ways. First, it decreases the exposed surface area of the body through which heat can be lost, thus decreasing the rate of loss. Second, it traps water close to the body, particularly around the chest and abdomen where the vital organs are located. Cross your legs below the knee and bring your knees up as far as your PFD will allow. Cross your arms around the front of your PFD or around your knees if you can reach that far.

This position works well with a PFD. If you do not have one, combine the HELP position with the relaxed floating technique. First take a deep breath while looking all around for opportunities to signal distress. Then shut your mouth and eyes and place your head below water. Bring your knees up to your chest, cross your ankles and hug your shins with your arms. Stay in this position until you need to draw another breath.

she is suffering from severe hypothermia and is in danger of falling into a coma.

Treatment should include warming the body slowly – you don't want to shock the person's system by rapid warming – with dry clothing and warm, nourishing drinks such as broth. (Avoid caffeinated coffee and tea because these are diuretics and prevent the body from absorbing needed warmth.

Avoid alcohol as it also lowers body temperature.) Do not give any drinks to someone who is suffering from severe hypothermia. All attempts should be made to remove the person from the exposed environment, including to an enclosed cabin or, if the boat is undecked, the bottom of the boat. Hot packs, applied around the neck, armpits, trunk, and between the legs, are especially helpful. If these are not available, a hypo-thermic person should be warmed with the warmth of another crew member through skin-to-skin contact. In such a case, wrap both people in dry blankets.

Administer first aid to the person, ensuring that the person is breathing normally – not taking short, shallow breaths – and that her pulse is normal. Professional help should be sought immediately if a person is severely hypothermic.

## SUNBURN

Sailors are especially prone to the risks of sun exposure – both, in the long term, from skin cancer and, in the short term, from sunburn. Always cover up. Extremities such as the nose, ears, backs of hands, and the back of the neck are vulnerable. Wear a broad-brimmed hat, with a strap under the chin, which will shade the head and neck. Wear long sleeves to protect the arms.

## DEHYDRATION

Prolonged exposure to the wind and sun conspires to dehydrate the human body. Even in cold temperatures, it is possible to become dangerously dehydrated. Drink water regularly – every 30 minutes or so – even if you are not thirsty.

## Requesting assistance

Once you are in a life raft, never give up hope that you will be saved. People have lived for months in the most improbable situations. Signal for help with all means available to you.

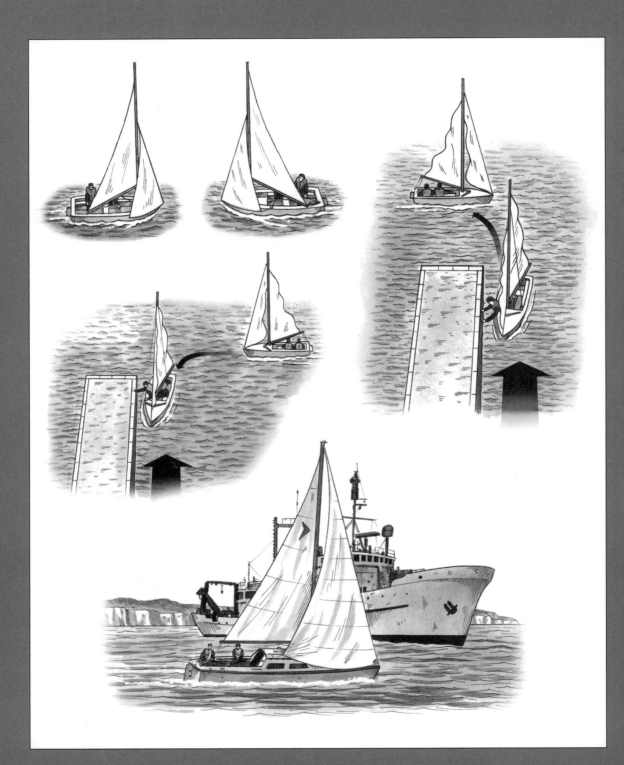

# CHAPTER 10

# Getting started

This chapter is dedicated to the person who cannot follow written instructions and needs to do whatever it is that needs doing in order to really learn how it's done. For even the quickest learner, however, there are some sailing fundamentals that should be considered before getting started.

I've heard countless stories of people who 'tried sailing once' and were frustrated because they could get the boat to go only one way, usually dead downwind, which meant that they soon became stranded and had to ask for a tow back to where they started.

A sailboat cannot sail straight into the wind – that is a fact. But many small sailboats can sail pretty close, about 30–40 degrees off the wind, so that progress can be made upwind by 'tacking' back and forth until the destination is achieved. What follows are a few more pointers on getting started. If some of the terms sound obscure, keep reading, as the term can usually be deciphered by its context – or refer to the glossary.

The first bit of information to establish is the direction of the wind. It will be blowing from three basic directions: onto the beach – onshore; off the beach – offshore; and parallel with the beach, from one direction or another. To determine the direction of the wind, face the wind and feel it blowing evenly across your ears. The direction your nose is pointed is called the 'eye' of the wind. If you're behind a group of buildings, dunes, or tall trees, the direction of the wind will be confused, seeming not to be blowing consistently from one direction. Once the boat is launched and away from this blocked area, called 'the lee', the wind will blow uninterrupted and can be quite strong.

Before heading out in these conditions, you should attempt to gain a clear sense of the wind's true direction and velocity. Walk to a hilltop or away from large buildings.

## Launching from a beach in a headwind

Getting off the beach will be a challenge in this scenario, as the wind and waves will attempt to push you back ashore. Once you have gained deep water, gain sea room by making tight tacks, keeping the sails in tight, and working your way gradually away from the beach. Getting back will be a whole lot easier.

Also, observe the direction that flags are blowing or the orientation of nearby boats at anchor or on moorings; they will be pointed into the wind.

## SAILING DINGHY

Let's say you're the proud new owner of a sailing dinghy that you will launch from a beach to start sailing right away. The boat has a 4m-long (14ft-long) planing hull and a daggerboard to counteract leeway, and it carries a mainsail and a jib on its single mast. It is steered by a tiller.

The most frustrating (or dangerous) wind for the beginning sailor is the offshore wind. It will be relatively easy for the skipper in this situation to get started, as the breeze will help to move the vessel into deep water and gain some room to manoeuvre. But the biggest challenge for the novice sailor is to sail efficiently 'close to the wind', which involves steering the vessel as close to the eye of the wind as possible, with the sails pulled in tightly, so as to make progress in the general direction of the wind. If the novice skipper is blown downwind by an offshore breeze, it will be a long 'beat' to get back to the position where he started. It's always easier to be pushed downwind than to make progress upwind.

### Wind blowing offshore

In this condition, the novice should gain deep water, so as not to foul the daggerboard in the shallows or be rolled by the surf, and then immediately turn the rudder to sail in a direction parallel with the shore. The wind will be coming over the vessel's beam, allowing good speed without getting pushed dangerously far from shore.

Once clear of shallow water, and thus armed with the knowledge of the wind's true direction and general velocity, deploy the daggerboard, dropping it down as far as possible. This will help drive the boat in a straight line. (It might be helpful to set the mainsail while the boat is on the beach. If so, launch the boat stern-first so that the sail will not fill and the boat sail off without you as you wade into the water.)

Once the mainsail is up, set the jib by hauling the halyard and making the line off securely to a cleat. Each of the sails should have a 'sheet', a line that is designated for the express purpose of adjusting the angle of the sail to the wind.

### Wind blowing onshore

In this condition, the challenge will be launching the boat and gaining deep water without being pushed back onto the beach. Set the mainsail and jib before you head out. They will flap uselessly – not keeping you from getting into the water – because the boat will be pointed right into the wind as you move it into the water. Once aboard, you'll need to perform a few tacks with the sails in tight, sailing as close to the eye of the wind as possible without the sails luffing. If the daggerboard is deployed and the sails are in tight, you should be able to sail to within 30–40 degrees of the wind's direction, thereby gaining deeper water.

### Wind blowing parallel to the beach

This is the best condition for getting started. Set the mainsail and jib before launching, but do not tie the sheets off. Allow the sails to luff. If they begin to draw before you are ready, the boat could take off without you or be pushed away from the direction you want it to launch.

Keep in mind that it's much easier to manoeuvre a sailboat in a direction that is away from the eye of the wind. For this reason, it makes sense to begin sailing towards the eye of the wind, saving the downwind manoeuvring for the return trip.

When landing on the beach at the end of your sailing adventure, remember to pull the daggerboard back up so that it does not touch bottom. Drop the sails as soon as you

## Getting back to shore

To return to shore in an onshore wind, douse the sails as you approach the beach. This will reduce your speed so you do not move too fast. Also, be sure to raise the daggerboard or centreboard, so that it does not foul on the bottom.

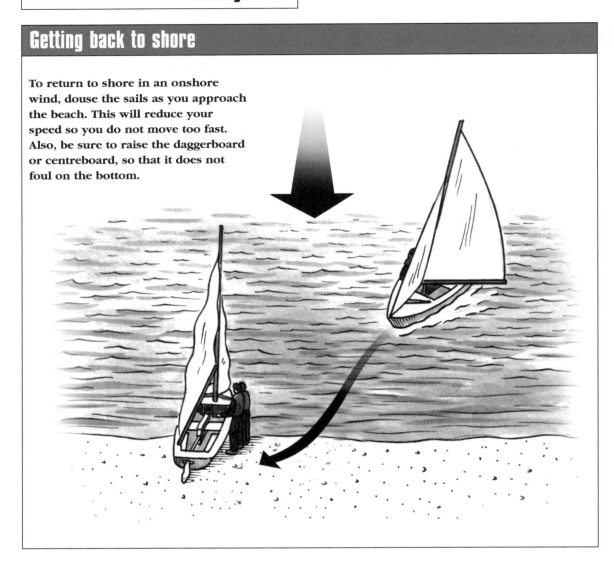

no longer need them for manoeuvring. Otherwise, they will flap annoyingly and add to the confusion.

## KEEL BOAT

You won't be able to launch a keel boat from the beach. Your new boat will probably be lying alongside a dock or on a mooring. To begin, let's assume your keel boat is 6m (20ft) long, has a small inboard motor, has a single mast

with a mainsail and a jib, and is steered by a tiller. The boat is hanging on a mooring.

As always, determine the direction that the wind is blowing. A good indicator is the direction the boat's bow is pointing. Unless the current in your area is severe, the boat will be pointing directly into the wind.

To get started, untie the boat's tiller. There are often small lashings around a tiller that are applied when the vessel is left on a mooring so that the rudder doesn't slop around. Once the rudder is free, secure the halyard to the head of the mainsail. The halyard, the line intended to raise the sail, should have a shackle that will need to be secured to the sail's topmost grommet. If there is no such hardware, tie a bowline through the sail's head.

Before raising the sail, remove the sail's 'sheet' from the cleats. The sheet is the line that will control the angle of the sail relative to the boat. If you do not release the sheet, the sail could fill with wind before you are ready for it to do so. Now you are ready to raise the sail; haul it all the way up, making it as tight as possible so that the sail actually stretches a little along the leading edge.

Now, do the same with the jib. Remove the lashings (or remove the sail from the bag and 'hank' it to the stay), then secure the

## Docking under sail

If you are returning to a dock under sail, you will need to 'round up' to take off way – or speed. Pick a dock that is directed the same as the wind, or release your sails as you approach if this is not an option.

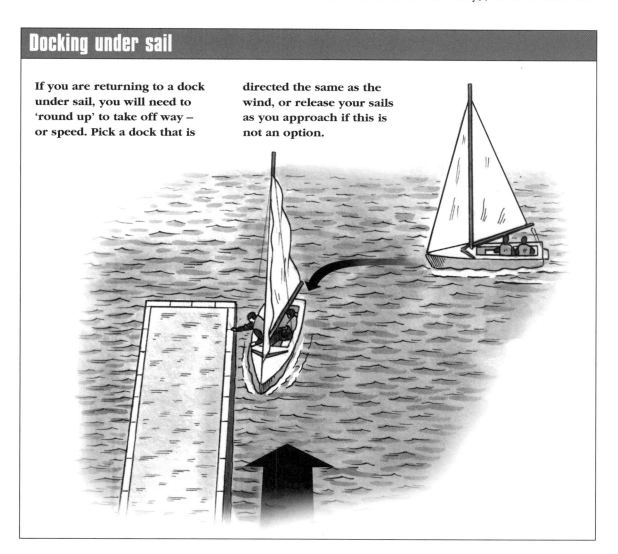

halyard in the same manner as the mainsail. Both the jib sheets will need to be secured as well. Tie them off on the sail's clew (the lower, after corner), and lead the other ends back to the cockpit in such a way that the lines will not foul on the shrouds. Try to picture in your mind how the sail will look when it is set. As with the mainsail, don't tie off the sheets to a cleat because you do not want the sail to fill – yet. Raise the jib, allowing the sails to flap in the breeze.

Before getting under way, ask yourself in which direction you would like the boat to sail. (The boat's location might mean initially that it can go in only one direction to gain open water.) The best way to get the boat pointing in the direction you would like is to have the jib backed so that it will push the bow in the right direction. This can be done by the person on the foredeck who will be slipping the mooring pennant, or it can be done in the cockpit by bringing in the correct jib sheet.

Imagine the wind as a giant finger that will be pushing your bow. Picture in your mind which side of the boat you'd like the wind's finger to push. When you are certain everything is in order, slip the mooring

## Sailing with kids

Children can enjoy sailing as much – or more – as any adult. Children as young as seven or eight years old are fully capable of learning the fundamentals of sailing, and many can learn how to handle a boat on their own. Some can learn to race competitively. The trick to getting children involved is to inspire them, give them the latitude to discover what it is about sailing that is appealing – impressing upon them the importance of being safe at the same time.

If they are young and easily distracted, consider bringing along diversionary toys that can be used to stave off boredom; a bored child on a sailboat is no fun for anyone, and he will likely not ever want to come back. Yet, if the child is engaged in certain activities that are appropriate for his age, his comfort on a boat will develop and likely lead to an appreciation of sailing.

Many children, depending on age and attention span, will respond to knot tying. A book that shows how to tie basic knots can be the perfect way to engage a child's inquisitive mind and capable fingers. Similarly, a book on basic navigation or sea adventures, fiction or nonfiction, can be a source of amazement to a child. Local guidebooks which include information on various points of interest along a route are another great way to involve a child in the progress of the boat.

An intense child, someone who is naturally competitive and physically advanced, will likely enjoy sailboat racing. Numerous yacht clubs and youth sailing groups offer diverse programs geared towards racing or other sailing styles.

When teaching a child about sailboats, emphasis should always be given to safety. Life jackets should always be worn, by both children and adults, at all times – aboard small boats especially. As discussed in the chapter on sailing equipment, a child's life jacket should be designated as appropriate for a child; a child will slip out of an adult life jacket if he goes overboard.

Many parents find success at inspiring their children to join them on a boat by having them invite their friends aboard. A child who would otherwise be bored will often find joy in sharing the uniqueness of a boat with a friend.

pennant from the cleat on the bow, and move carefully back to the cockpit. (If you're not alone, have another crew member slip the pennant off when you say you are ready.)

As the boat slips away from the mooring, the jib filling on one side, gradually bring the mainsail in tight. Using the tiller, attempt to steady the vessel's course on a distant object. The first challenge will be to maintain a steady course. You don't want the boat to weave erratically. Check by glancing back at the boat's wake and seeing how straight a path you are carving through the water.

You will want the sails to be drawing efficiently. Adjust the sails' angles by using the sheets. (For further details on how to trim sails, refer a more extensive discussion in Chapter 7.)

To return to your mooring, try to approach on a beam reach – with the wind coming across your deck at a perpendicular angle. You'll want to turn the boat up into the wind and allow the boat to coast to a stop right at the mooring. How far will your boat coast as you turn into the wind? Only practice will show you; you might take a few trial runs on another mooring or on another soft object that is fixed to the

## Getting under way from a dock

To get under way by sail power, raise the sails with the bow pointed into the wind. Slip the vessel free of the dock, and allow the sails to fill. This will gain speed and steerage.

# Trimming your sails

When trimming the sails, you want the sails to be full and drawing, not flapping or 'luffing'. But you don't want them to be too tight, which is inefficient.

A. When adjusting the trim, find that magic spot that is created when you are on the course you want (parallel with the shore, for example) and the sails are luffing a little.

B. Now, using the sheets, draw them in gently one at a time until the sails stop luffing. This is the optimal angle for the sails for a given heading.

C. If you want to reverse direction, turn the tiller to bring the bow through the eye of the wind so that the sails fill on the other side of the boat. This is called a 'tack'.

D. Once through the tack, you'll need to cross the jib by untying one sheet and securing the other.

E. Once on the heading you desire, perform the same 'luff test', easing the sails until they luff, then bringing them back in just enough to stop the luffing.

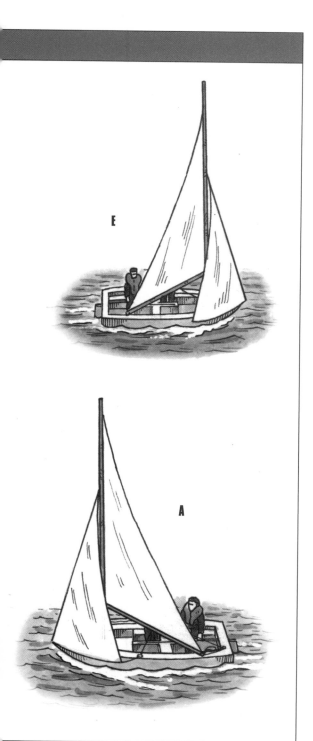

bottom. Once the boat has coasted to a stop, use a boathook to grab the mooring pennant and bring the eye aboard. It might help to have already dropped the jib so that it is not in the way during this manoeuvre. Once aboard, place the mooring eye around the bow cleat. It might be necessary to tie another tag line onto the heavier mooring pennant as extra security. You've made it!

Drop the mainsail and stow the sails carefully. If the jib comes off the stay, fold it carefully and return it to its bag. Be sure to securely tie the mainsail with sail ties and cover it. The sun's rays will seriously damage the sails over a surprisingly short period of time. Before leaving the boat, be sure all that all the lines (halyards and sheets) are secured to their respective coils and coiled properly.

## RULES OF THE ROAD

Every boat should be equipped with a book that details the Nautical Rules of the Road. These books are published by government agencies and private publishers. It is imperative that every skipper knows the rules that apply to the motion of her boat on the water. Ignorance of the rules is not a defence in a court of law, and failure to follow the rules can result in serious fines. Most importantly, however, sailing without this knowledge is dangerous. You will be sharing the waterways with other vessels, many of which will be large commercial vessels that will be piloted in strict adherence to the rules. By knowing the rules – at least those few that govern rights of way pertaining to your vessel – and by applying common sense, dangerous circumstances can be avoided.

The following is not a complete list of the nautical rules. It is an introduction to some of the rules that affect the navigation of small boats. Every nation has somewhat different rules; however, many adhere to the basic structure of the International Rules as prescribed by the International Maritime Organization (IMO).

- Keep a proper lookout. Scanning the horizon at regular intervals is the best way to describe a lookout's role. Other vessels can enter a boat's space at surprising speed. Even if your own boat is incapable of speeds greater than nine or ten knots, many commercial vessels travel at well over 20 knots, while recreational power-boats may travel at over 40 knots. Look over your shoulder frequently; even if a vessel that is overtaking you is burdened to stay out of your way, you should be aware of its presence. It is your responsibility to maintain a steady course. Peek frequently below the sails so that you gain a clear view of what may be lying ahead.

- Give way to all commercial traffic. There are no laws stating that large commercial vessels have right of way over small

## Keep lookout

You will share the water with numerous other boats. Always give way to large commercial vessels. Although a sailboat has right of way over power-driven vessels, common courtesy dictates that recreational vessels give way to those that are working on the water, including fishing vessels, government vessels, tankers, container ships, and tugboats.

# Sailing at night

Sailing at night is an exciting and rewarding adventure. All the same rules apply – of safety, vigilance, and careful watchkeeping practices – but the operations must be carried on in the dark. You will not be able to accurately judge distances at night, making 'eyeball' navigation all but impossible. Radar, depthsounders, and GPS units are especially helpful for night navigation, but not absolutely necessary. A solid understanding of use of the compass for accurate chart navigation is necessary, however, so that you can keep track of your boat's position and progress through the water.

Pay careful attention to the weather forecast. Rain, fog, and haze will diminish visibility further, turning what might be an otherwise peaceful sail into a stressful experience. For your first night sail, pick a clear night, preferably a moonlit night. Note where all hazards on your trip will be, including rocks, shoals, unlit points of land, and even unlit buoys. If you are planning to use a buoy as a navigational aid, and the buoy is not lit, take extra care not to run into it. Numerous vessels have found buoys the hard way, especially if their crew have been navigating by GPS and plugging in the numbers as waypoints.

This brings up the most important consideration when sailing at night: the look-out. While during daylight hours a lookout is a critical position, non-stop vigilance is required at night. As distances are extremely difficult to determine in the dark, you will need early warning of the existence of other objects. Scan the horizon frequently for lights and other objects. Keep track of your position every hour or every half hour (or less) if you are navigating close to land.

Write out a set of 'night orders', instructions for each crew member to follow that describes to them how they should maintain the boat during their watch if the skipper is going to get some sleep. Explain in the night orders the importance of keeping a lookout and waking the skipper in the event of any doubt or confusion. Lookouts should watch for the running lights of other vessels. By seeing another's red or green sidelights, and keeping track of their relative bearing over time (several minutes), one should be able to figure out an estimate of the other vessel's course and speed.

In general, extra precaution should be taken on all counts when preparing for a night sail. But this should not detract from the enjoyment.

recreational ones, but it is common courtesy – and good sense – to give way to all commercial traffic. A 300-m (1000-ft) container ship or tanker moving at 15 or 20 knots is far more difficult to manoeuvre than your 6-m (20-ft) sailboat. Get out of the way, and do so early to ensure that there is no confusion at the last minute.

- Small ferries, tugboats, and fishing vessels (whether or not they're fishing) should be treated with the same respect. Give

them a wide berth; if you see that your course could create a 'close quarters' situation a few minutes down the line, adjust your course in an obvious way so that the captain will have no doubt that you have altered course. The crew of these vessels working on the water are often under tremendous pressure to maintain tight schedules.

- Note, too, that the law does give priority to vessels that are constrained to their course by their deep draft.

# Coastal voyage planning

Planning a voyage of any length, either for one day or several, should start at home the night before – or earlier if the voyage is lengthy. First, gather the necessary charts for your planned destination(s). Consider the fact that the weather may not be as forecasted, making it a good idea to carry charts that are adjacent to the area you plan on visiting. You'll be glad you did if your voyage changes.

Listen to the weather forecast and write down what it says. (Listen again in the morning as it may have changed.) Note the times of the tides and their height – if applicable. Based on the anticipated wind speeds and direction, lay down your expected passage plan, including the course – drawn in pencil – and note the distances between prominent points. You should have a sense of how fast your boat can travel in the wind predicted. Be conservative in your estimates, but include destinations and routes in your plans that account for both slower and faster speeds.

If you have a handheld GPS unit, enter the waypoints of your passage plan on the unit. The GPS will then offer compass courses to waypoints as they are achieved, easing the burden of navigational responsibilities and contributing to your situational awareness.

All of this information – weather forecast, expected routes and mileage, intended destinations – should be entered into the boat's logbook. You will then be able to refer to it during the voyage, updating it as necessary. When you log your journey, be sure to note the times that you actually achieved points along the way. By comparing predicted times and positions with actual ones, you will be able to fine tune your planning next time.

Document your expected journey on a separate sheet of paper, and give it to someone who is not going on the trip. Include the time you expect to return. This is called your 'float plan', and it will enable others to assist in a search in the event that you do not return at the anticipated time. Include a description of the boat (length of the hull, colour of the hull, and a rig description) and the number (and names) of people who will be on board. If you will be carrying a cell phone, be sure to include your number, but note on the float plan if you expect to be out of range at any point. Filing a float plan for a day's trip may sound like overkill, but it will save unnecessary hours, risk, and expense in the event that you need outside assistance.

## Fishing vessels

Fishing vessels engaged in fishing have a right of way over sailboats under sail. Fishing vessels will move erratically, often turning in circles and even backing down. Fishing vessels also often have long nets that are deployed over the side. They should not be approached, and extreme caution should be used when passing these vessels. While fishing vessel skippers are also required to keep a sharp lookout, their attention is often focused on their work, which takes place on deck and in the waters close to their vessel's sides. They may not be scanning the horizon as carefully as you.

## Tugs and towboats

Tugboats towing or pushing barges are an extreme hazard to recreational vessels. When pushing a barge ahead, visibility in the tug's wheelhouse is extremely limited. If you cannot see the vessel's wheelhouse from where you are in the water, then the crew aboard the tug cannot see you. Don't rely on the fact that they have radar: small, fibreglass and wooden vessels are often impossible to detect on all but the most sensitive radar sets, especially if there is any swell running.

A tugboat towing a barge will have a long wire or rope hawser dropping off its stern, which connects to the bow of the barge on a heavy bridle. The lines are not visible at the surface. The line is there, sometimes more than 300m (1000ft) long, but it is below the sea surface. Never attempt to cross between these two vessels – that is, the tug and the barge– as your boat will be 'tripped' by the towline. Extreme caution should always be used around tug and barge combinations.

## Sailboats

Sailboats typically enjoy right of way over other vessels, notwithstanding the above exceptions, but there are a few rules that apply between sailboats. These are fairly simple.

A sailboat on a port tack is burdened to stay out of the way of a sailboat on a starboard tack. Remember: starboard stay; port give way.

A sailboat that is overtaking another sailboat is burdened to stay out of the way of the vessel being overtaken.

In the case of two sailboats being on the same tack, the vessel that is to windward (upwind) of the leeward sailboat is burdened to give way.

There are several jingles that will help you to remember this, including the commonly heard 'POWs have no rights'. P stands for the vessel on the Port tack; O, for the vessel Overtaking; and W, for the vessel that is to Windward.

## ENGINE CARE

The most important maintenance schedule you can perform on your inboard diesel engine is changing the lubricating oil (and oil and fuel filters) regularly. Consult your engine manual for exact recommendations about how frequently this should be performed. Always change the oil after bringing the engine up to its full operating temperature. The oil will be made less viscous by heating – and therefore be easier to drain or pump – but it will also suspend any impurities in the oil instead of allowing them to settle in the bottom of the oil pan.

At the very least, change your engine oil once per season. Better yet, change it during the middle of your boating season and at the end, prior to putting it to bed for the winter.

Even if you consider yourself a sailor, don't ignore your engine. If you want it to operate trouble-free, take the time to get to know it. Perform an engine check at least once per day. Remove the engine's cover, then check the oil level, transmission fluid level, coolant level, and tightness of the belts. Next, clean the engine with paper towels or a damp cloth with mild detergent. If your engine is clean, you will notice any fluid leaks early, especially if you are inspecting it on a regular basis.

Look, listen, smell, and feel. You don't need to be a diesel mechanic to sense change – whether it is in the form of an odd smell, unusually coloured smoke coming from the exhaust, odd noises, or loose components.

Log all your maintenance, whether large changes or simple ones such as oil and filter changes. Note the engine hours each time you do this. Label all your systems' hoses with permanent marker in large type. Indicate the direction of flow with arrows.

Know your limits: if you sense trouble, take the time to work your way through basic troubleshooting. If this meets with no success, seek professional help. Engine mechanics have the specialized tools and knowledge to keep your engine running well.

# Further reading

**This book is just a beginning, to inspire the inexperienced sailor: there is a trove of literature available, to both the nautical neophyte and the expert sailor.**

The wonderful thing about sailing is that you never stop learning, whether you're sailing a Sunfish on a pond or preparing to cross an ocean on a 12-m (40-ft) sloop. Below are listed titles that will take your level of understanding up a notch, enabling you to delve deeper into the fascinating world of the ocean and boats.

Each of the books listed below are available at bookstores, through online sales, or at local libraries. Indeed, several of the books have been published many times since their initial printing, sometimes by more than one publisher; offered next to each title is the name of the publisher of the most recent edition.

**Adkins, Jan.**
*The Craft of Sail.*
New York: Walker & Co, 1973.

Perhaps the most lucid – and engaging – introduction to the beauty and mechanics of sailing, this book has been inspiring sailors for 30 years. Jan Adkins' alluring ink-wash drawings have a life of their own and make the mechanics of sailing – the concepts of the air foil, or how the power of the wind propels a boat through the water – a joy to learn. Included is a concise section on seamanship, anchoring, navigation, reefing, and line handling.

**Ashley, Clifford W.**
*The Ashley Book of Knots.*
New York: Doubleday, 1993.

Clifford Ashley, one of the most well-known maritime artists of the twentieth century, became fascinated with knots, eventually compiling what is still the most comprehensive collection of knots, bends, and hitches. Each knot is accompanied by Ashley's drawings, often in series. This is the definitive volume on knot-tying.

**Calder, Nigel.**
*Boatowner's Mechanical & Electrical
Manual: How to Maintain, Repair and
Improve Your Boat's Essential Systems.*
Camden, Maine: International Marine/
McGraw Hill, 1996.

Calder's manual has long been considered
the bible for recreational boat owners who
want to equip and maintain their vessels
with electrical and mechanical systems.
Calder, an Englishman living in the United
States, has made a name for himself with the
world's many sailing magazines as a well-
respected electrical and mechanical wizard.
He and his family have cruised extensively in
the Caribbean and along the United States'
East Coast in their cutter *Nada*, producing
cruising guides and articles the whole way.

**Carr, Michael W.**
*Weather Predicting Simplified.*
Camden, Maine: International Marine/
McGraw Hill, 1999.

Good weather books for the mariner are hard
to find. Michael Carr's book combines good
sea sense with weather information for the
recreational sailor. The author is a former
training schooner captain and an instructor
at a US maritime academy, and he is therefore
accustomed to teaching obscure subjects to
willing students. He devotes a good portion
of the book to explaining how modern technology (computers and the Internet) can
provide good access to raw weather sources.
Most importantly, he arms the reader with
the tools to interpret this information.

**Chapman, Charles Frederic and Elbert
S Maloney.**
*Chapman Piloting.*
New York: Sterling Publications, 1999.

*Chapman Piloting* is a classic, and more
than 60 editions have now been published. It
represents the establishment view of yachting,
including all the traditional Morse Code and
flag signal dressings, but it is also a useful
study guide for anyone wishing to pursue a
captain's or yachtmaster licence. It contains
excellent diagrams and explanations on handling small boats under power – invaluable
information for the novice boat owner. While
many of these books can be found in old
editions, the many new technologies make it
advisable to consult the latest edition.

**Coote, Jack.**
*Total Loss.*
London: Adlard Coles Nautical, 2001.

This book is a collection of first-hand
accounts of yachts that were lost to the sea.
Skippers and crew members describe the
voyages on which their vessels eventually
succumbed to the sea – whether as a result
of storms, navigation errors, or collision. If
there can be wisdom found in the mistakes
and misfortune of others, it is surely contained in this book. Most of the vessels were
lost in the years before the age of high-speed
communication and satellite navigation systems. This makes the book a priceless trove
of seamanship knowledge, as it details crews
exercising skilful means of handling yachts
in distress – skills that are all but vanishing in
this world of instant communication and
helicopter rescue.

**Gerr, Dave.**
*The Nature of Boats.*
Camden, Maine: International Marine, 1992.

Dave Gerr, a New York-based naval architect,
presents the broad spectrum of boating
know-how to any reader interested in
learning all the facts and figures of nautical
engineering. Included is all one would ever
need to know about powering a boat, hull
shape, the mechanics of stability, outboard
motors – and just about anything else. Gerr is

a details-oriented person, and his book, which includes information on both power and sailboats, is a complete analysis of nautical engineering. This is a fine book, and Gerr's sense of humour keeps the dense information moving along.

## Hartog, Jan de.
*The Captain.*
London: New English Library, 1978.

This novel by the Dutch-Canadian author Jan de Hartog is perhaps a bit out of place in this list of how-to books. But contained in its pages is perhaps the most poignant representation of what it means to command a vessel – whether you are skipper of a 4-m (12-ft) dinghy or, as in the case of this book, a muscular oceangoing tugboat. De Hartog's hero, Martinus Harinxma, is thrust, somewhat unwillingly, into the command of a tug at a young age, charged with manoeuvring ships and barges around the North Sea and eventually on the Murmansk Run during World War II. His character rises to the challenge, developing a kindly, if detached, approach to handling a vessel in the most extreme circumstances.

## Pardey, Lin and Larry.
*Cruising in Serrafyn.*
Dobbs Ferry, New York: Sheridan House, 1992.
— *Capable Cruiser.*
Middletown, California: Paradise Cay Publications, 1995.
— *Storm Tactics Handbook.*
Vista, California: Pardey Books, 1995.

If you're considering long-term voyaging – or just like reading about such voyages – these three books will provide both information and adventure. Lyn and Larry Pardey have been cruising the world's oceans for more than 30 years aboard engineless, wooden vessels, which they built themselves – first *Serrafyn*, a 7-m (24-ft) cutter, then the 8.5-m (28-ft) *Taleisin*, which they still sail. They believe in the integrity of traditional vessels, including deep, displacement hulls and tall gaff-topsail rigs. Their seamanship skills are second to none, and their advice on how to handle a little boat at sea has been learnt while sailing hundreds of thousands of sea miles and through countless storms. Most recently, in 2002, the couple rounded Cape Horn, testing many of their storm tactics. They have since produced a video, called *Storm Tactics*, in which they explain their methods. It is available for purchase on their website: www.landlpardey.com.

The Pardeys are steadfast proponents of 'heaving to' when storms are severe enough to threaten the safety of a boat that is either moving too fast and threatening to broach or is caught beam to the seas. The Pardeys maintain that any vessel that is built for ocean sailing can be made to heave to by experimenting with sail configuration and – if conditions deteriorate to the extreme – by deploying a sea anchor on a bridle off the bow.

## Rousmaniere, John.
*The Annapolis Book of Seamanship.*
New York: Simon & Schuster, 1999.

John Rousmaniere was a crew member in the devastating Fastnet storm of 1979, in which numerous yachts were destroyed and 15 lives lost. (He detailed the events of that yacht race in his gripping book *Fastnet, Force 10*, published by W.W. Norton.) He has been writing about issues of seamanship, storms, and safety at sea ever since. *The Annapolis Book of Seamanship* is the most comprehensive tome on sailing available – the definitive volume, indeed – and includes chapters on hull forms, seamanship, safety, weather, survival, navigation, and storm tactics. While some of the information borders on the arcane, it is nonetheless an impressive achievement and belongs on every yachtsman's bookshelf for quick reference. Rousmaniere is also an accomplished storyteller, making the reading engaging – and far less tedious – than many other reference books.

## Smith, Hervey Garrett.
*The Arts of the Sailor.*
London: Constable, 1990.

Working rope into knots, splices, and decoration is the perfect way to while away the hours on a boat. Smith's detailed sketches and descriptions walk the reader through the motions simply and purposefully. Perhaps the most valuable section is the chapter on splicing, which includes a series of drawings and explanations that are most useful when learning how to splice three-strand rope – a basic seamanship skill that is fairly straightforward, but can be tricky to master.

## Farnsworth, B.A. and Young, Larry C.
*Nautical Rules of the Road.*
Westbranch, Iowa: Tidewater
Publishers, 1990.

A Rules of the Road book (pertaining to the appropriate country) should be standard equipment on each vessel. As governing agencies are fond of saying, ignorance of the rules is not an excuse in the event of an accident. It is your responsibility to know them all, including the obligations of your vessel in manoeuvres around others, sound signals, lights, and day shapes. The best way to learn the rules is to buy a book, read it through several times, then refer to it several times over the course of the boating season. Many editions of the Rules book include quick-reference guides designed for the recreational boat owner.

## Bowditch, Nathaniel
*The New American Practical Navigator.*
Middletown, California: Paradise Cay
Publications, 2002.

The *American Practical Navigator* was first written by a genius lad from Massachusetts called Nathaniel Bowditch, a mathematician who singlehandedly opened the secretive world of navigation, previously accessible only to officers, to anyone who cared to learn it. The book, which has come to be known as Bowditch, has been in print for more than 200 years, having gone through nearly countless edits and developments to account for continuing changes in technology and custom.

Bowditch remains an invaluable volume for both recreational and merchant seamen. It includes sections on navigation, seamanship, weather, and numerous tables for deriving just about anything. Since 1995, it has been published in one volume. A bicentennial edition was published in 2002.

### SAILING COURSES
If you wish to take an introductory sailing course, or need advice or information on anything to do with sailing, here are a few URLs that will help:

- In the United Kingdom, try the Royal Yachting Association homepage: www.rya.org.uk
- In the United States, try: www.ussailing.org
- In Australia, try the Australian Yachting Federation homepage: www.yachting.org.au
- Or for a comprehensive listing of national authorities: www.sailing.org/mna/mna.asp

# Glossary

**Abaft:** a direction indicating something 'aft of' another object

**Abeam:** a direction indicating an object that is at a right angle to the vessel's widest point, its beam

**Aloft:** up in the rigging

**Athwartships:** a direction perpendicular to a boat's centreline

**Bar:** the point where a river meets the sea. This is an area that can pose extreme risk to the sailboat because of large, steep waves that form as a result of conflicting currents

**Barometer:** an instrument used in weather forecasting for measuring surface pressure

**Beam:** a vessel's widest point

**Beaufort Scale:** a system of estimating the force of the wind by reading the surface of the water and seeing the wind's effects in making waves

**Belowdecks:** a vessel's cabin areas

**Bitter end:** the end of a line that is not attached to anything

**Block (pulley):** a piece of equipment used for providing mechanical advantage, consisting of a set of cheeks, a sheave, and bearings

**Bulwarks:** the side of a ship above deck

**Cat:** a vessel whose rig consists of a mainsail and no jib

**Catamaran:** a two-hulled vessel

**Centreboard:** a pivoting board that is housed in a trunk used for counteracting the effects of leeway

**Cleat:** a horned deck or dock fitting for securing a line

**Clew:** the bottom, aft-most corner of a sail

**Confused sea:** a dangerous sea state – often brought on by shifting winds or found in an area of converging currents – that includes no discernible pattern of waves and swells

**Course:** the direction that a vessel is travelling through the water

**Daggerboard:** a board that is raised up and down in a trunk used for counteracting the effects of leeway

**Displacement hull:** a hull form that is intended to ride through the water, as opposed to a planing hull, which skims the surface

**Downhaul:** a line used for bringing down a sail

**Ebb:** the outgoing tide, as in ebb tide or ebb current

**EPIRB:** Emergency position indicating radio beacon, an emergency device used for contacting rescue agencies

**Fair lead:** when a line is set up so as to minimize chafe

**Fetch:** a linear distance over the surface of water when discussing the effects of wind on the height of waves – for example, one-mile fetch or unlimited fetch.

**Flare:** a signalling device that can be projected into the sky

**Flood:** the incoming tide, as in flood tide or flood current

**Foot:** the bottom length of a sail

**Gaff:** a spar that secures the peak and throat of a sail on a gaff-rigged vessel

**Gaff rig:** a vessel with gaff sail(s)

**Gybe:** to turn the vessel so that the stern passes through the direction of the wind

**Halyard:** a line used to haul up a sail

**Handy-billy:** a portable system of blocks and line used for gaining mechanical advantage

**Head:** 1. the uppermost corner of a sail
2. a marine toilet

**Heading:** the direction a vessel's bow is pointing

**Heave:** one of the six degrees of motion, indicating a motion straight up or down

**Helm:** a boat's steering wheel

**Jib:** a triangular sail set on a vessel's bow

**Keel:** a fixed protrusion beneath the hull, used for counteracting the effects of leeway

**Ketch:** a rig style that features two masts, the larger one forward and the smaller (called the mizzen) aft

**Leeboards:** a pair of boards deployed over either side of some sailing vessels, used to counteract the effects of leeway

**Leech:** the after-most edge of a sail

**Leeway:** a side-slipping force

**Leeward:** the side of a vessel or other object that is protected from the wind

**Life raft:** an emergency raft used for flotation

**Luff:** 1. (noun) the forward, or leading, edge of a sail 2. (verb) the flogging motion of a sail that is not properly shaped into a foil by the wind

**Mainsail:** the largest of a vessel's sails

**Mizzen:** on a ketch or a yawl, the after-most sail (or mast)

**Multihull:** either a catamaran or trimaran

**Neap tide:** a phenomenon caused by the moon and sun being out of alignment with the earth, resulting in lower high tides and higher low tides. (See also SPRING TIDE)

**Pitch:** one of the six degrees of motion, the hobby-horsing motion of a vessel

**Planing hull:** a hull designed to skim the surface of the water

**Port:** when facing forward, the left side of a vessel

**Quadrant:** part of certain steering systems, this is the section that is secured to the top of the rudder

**Quarter:** the aft-most corners of a vessel, specifically the port and starboard quarters

**Reef points:** small lines that serve to tie up the base of a sail when reefing

**Reef outhaul:** a line that is used for reefing. It attaches to a cringle in the leach of a sail and is reeved through a block on the end of the boom at the clew

**Roll:** one of the six degrees of motion, a side-to-side motion

**Rudder:** a part of a vessel's steering system that protrudes into the water, turned by a tiller or helm

**Rules of the Road:** the international set of rules meant to assist in the safe navigation of vessels

**Running rigging:** the lines that are used to handle sail

**Schooner:** a rig that features the mainmast aft and the smaller (called the foremast) forward

**Seacock:** a valve used in a hull for securing hoses, such as for a sink, engine cooling system, or marine toilet

**Sheave:** the round, wheel-like section of a block that turns on bearings

**Sheet:** a line used for adjusting the trim of a sail

**Snatch-block:** a block that can be opened to capture a line without needing to pass through the bitter end. Snatch blocks are often used as fair leads for sheets

**Sound signal:** a device such as a horn or bell used for signalling other vessels

**Spring tide:** a phenomenon caused when the sun and moon are aligned with the earth, which creates higher than normal high tides and lower than normal low tides

**Stanchion:** the vertical support for a lifeline

**Standing end:** the end of a line that is attached to something

**Standing rigging:** wire rigging that supports the mast

**Starboard:** when looking forward, the right-hand side of a vessel

**Steerageway:** when a vessel is moving through the water at a rate that allows it to be steered by its rudder

**Surge:** one of the six degrees of motion, surge is when a vessel is pushed directly ahead or astern

**Sway:** one of the six degrees of motion, sway is when a vessel is moved to one side or another

**Tack:** 1. (noun) the forward corner of the foot of a sail. 2. (verb) to turn the vessel so that the bow passes through the wind

**Through-hull:** also known as a seacock

**Tide:** the vertical rise and fall of the water as a result of the effects of gravity imposed by the moon and, to a lesser degree, the sun

**Tidal current:** horizontal movement of water as a result of the tide

**Tiller:** a lever used for turning the rudder

**Topping lift:** a line used to adjust the height of a boom

**Trimaran:** a multihull vessel with three hulls

**Under way:** when a vessel is not secured to a fixed object such as a dock, mooring, or anchor. A vessel adrift is under way

**Vang:** a system of lines and blocks that connects from the boom to the base of the mast used for controlling the angle of the boom

**Windward:** the side of an object that is facing the direction of the wind

**Yaw:** one of the six degrees of motion, a corkscrew-like motion of the hull

**Yawl:** a rig style that has the larger mast (the mainmast) forward and a smaller mast (the mizzen) aft. A yawl is different from a ketch because the mizzenmast is positioned abaft the vessel's rudder post

# Index